What People Are S   Threshold Bible Study

"Here, at last, is a Bible study for those of us who don't like Bible studies! Rather than focusing on a book, Stephen Binz invites us to view many well-known passages through the lens of a particular theme, bringing new meaning to the passages and a deeper connection to the theme in our own lives. His discussions do far more than inform; they ask for commitment and assent on the part of the reader/prayer."

Kathleen O'Connell Chesto, author of F.I.R.E. and *Why Are the Dandelions Weeds?*

"God's Holy Word addresses the deepest levels of our lives with the assurance of divine grace and wisdom for our individual and communal faith. I am grateful for this new series introducing God's people to the riches of Sacred Scripture. May these guides to understanding the great truths of our redemption bring us all closer to the Lord of our salvation."

Most Reverend Timothy M. Dolan, Archbishop of Milwaukee

"Threshold Bible Study provides an introduction to some major biblical themes, enabling Catholics to read, with greater understanding, the Bible in the Church. When studied along with the documents of Vatican II and the *Catechism of the Catholic Church*, this series can be a help for personal and group Bible study."

Francis Cardinal George, O.M.I., Archbishop of Chicago

"Threshold Bible Study offers a marvelous new approach for individuals and groups to study themes in our rich biblical and theological tradition. Moving through these thematic units feels like gazing at panels of stained glass windows, viewing similar images through different lights."

John Endres, S.J., professor of Scripture, Jesuit School of Theology, Berkeley

"Threshold Bible Study offers solid scholarship and spiritual depth. Drawing on the Church's living Tradition and the Jewish roots of the New Testament, Threshold Bible Study can be counted on for lively individual study and prayer, even while it offers spiritual riches to deepen communal conversation and reflection among the people of God."

Scott Hahn, professor of biblical theology,
Franciscan University of Steubenville

"The distance many feel between the Word of God and their everyday lives can be overwhelming. It need not be so. Threshold Bible Study is a fine blend of the best of biblical scholarship and a realistic sensitivity to the spiritual journey of the believing Christian. I recommend it highly."

Francis J. Moloney, S.D.B., The Katharine Drexel Professor of Religious Studies, The Catholic University of America, Washington, D.C.

"Stephen Binz offers an invaluable guide that can make reading the Bible enjoyable (again) and truly nourishing. A real education on how to read the Bible, this series prepares people to discuss Scripture and to share it in community."

Jacques Nieuviarts, Professor of Scripture, Institut Catholique de Toulouse, France

"Threshold Bible Study is a refreshing approach to enable participants to ponder the Scriptures more deeply. The thematic material is clearly presented with a mix of information and spiritual nourishment. The questions are thoughtful and the principles for group discussion are quite helpful. This series provides a practical way for faithful people to get to know the Bible better and to enjoy the fruits of biblical prayer."

Irene Nowell, O.S.B., Mount St. Scholastica, Atchison, Kansas, Editorial committee for Old Testament translation of the *New American Bible*

"Threshold Bible Study is appropriately named, for its commentary and study questions bring people to the threshold of the text and invite them in. The questions guide but do not dominate. They lead readers to ponder and wrestle with the biblical passages and take them across the threshold toward life with God. Stephen Binz's work stands in the tradition of the biblical renewal movement and brings it back to life. We need more of this in the Church."

Kathleen M. O'Connor, professor of Old Testament, Columbia Theological Seminary

"I most strongly recommend Stephen Binz's Threshold Bible Study for adult Bible classes, religious education, and personal spiritual enrichment. The series is exceptional for its scholarly solidity, pastoral practicality, and clarity of presentation. The Church owes Binz a great debt of gratitude for his generous and competent labor in the service of the Word of God."

Peter C. Phan, Ignacio Ellacuría Professor of Catholic Social Thought, Georgetown University

"Written in a clear and concise style, Threshold Bible Study presents solid contemporary biblical scholarship, offers questions for reflection and/or discussion, and then demonstrates a way to pray from the Scriptures. All these elements work together to offer the reader a wonderful insight into how the sacred texts of our faith can touch our lives in a profound and practical way today. I heartily recommend this series to both individuals and to Bible study groups."

Abbot Gregory J. Polan, O.S.B., Conception Abbey and Seminary College

The NAMES of JESUS

Stephen J. Binz

Third printing 2010

The content and format of this study has been adapted from material previously published in *God's Word Today* magazine.

The Scripture passages contained herein are from the *New Revised Standard Version of the Bible,* Catholic edition. Copyright ©1989, by the Division of Christian Education of the National Council of Churches in the U.S.A. All rights reserved.

TWENTY-THIRD PUBLICATIONS
A Division of Bayard
One Montauk Avenue, Suite 200
New London, CT 06320
(860) 437-3012 or (800) 321-0411
www.23rdpublications.com
ISBN 978-1-58595-315-8

Library of Congress Catalog Card Number: 2006928080
Printed in the U.S.A.

Contents

LESSONS 13–18

LESSONS 19–24

LESSONS 25–30

How to Use
Threshold Bible Study

E ach book in the Threshold Bible Study series is designed to lead you through a new doorway of biblical awareness, to accompany you across a unique threshold of understanding. The characters, places, and images that you encounter in each of these topical studies will help you explore fresh dimensions of your faith and discover richer insights for your spiritual life.

Threshold Bible Study covers biblical themes in depth in a short amount of time. Unlike more traditional Bible studies that treat a biblical book or series of books, Threshold Bible Study aims to address specific topics within the entire Bible. The goal is not for you to comprehend everything about each passage, but rather for you to understand what a variety of passages from different books of the Bible reveals about the topic of each study.

Threshold Bible Study offers you an opportunity to explore the entire Bible from the viewpoint of a variety of themes. The commentary that follows each biblical passage launches your reflection about that passage and helps you begin to see its significance within the context of your contemporary experience. The questions following the commentary challenge you to understand the passage more fully and apply it to your own life. The prayer starter helps conclude your study by integrating learning into your relationship with God.

These studies are designed for maximum flexibility. Each study is presented in a workbook format, with sections for reading, reflecting, writing, discussing, and praying. Space for writing after each question is ideal for personal study and allows group members to prepare in advance for their discussion. The thirty lessons in each topic may be used by an individual over the period of a month, or by a group for six sessions, with lessons to be studied each week before the next group meeting. These studies are ideal for Bible study groups, small Christian communities, adult faith formation, student groups, Sunday school, neighborhood groups, and family reading, as well as for individual learning.

The method of Threshold Bible Study is rooted in the classical tradition of *lectio divina,* an ancient yet contemporary means for reading the Scriptures reflectively and prayerfully. Reading and interpreting the text (*lectio*) is followed by reflective meditation on its message (*meditatio*). This reading and reflecting flows into prayer from the heart (*oratio* and *contemplatio*).

This ancient method assures us that Bible study is a matter of both the mind and the heart. It is not just an intellectual exercise to learn more and be able to discuss the Bible with others. It is, more importantly, a transforming experience. Reflecting on God's word, guided by the Holy Spirit, illumines the mind with wisdom and stirs the heart with zeal.

Following the personal Bible study, Threshold Bible Study offers a method for extending *lectio divina* into a weekly conversation with a small group. This communal experience will allow participants to enhance their appreciation of the message and build up a spiritual community (*collatio*). The end result will be to increase not only individual faith, but also faithful witness in the context of daily life (*operatio*).

Through the spiritual disciplines of Scripture reading, study, reflection, conversation, and prayer, you will experience God's grace more abundantly as your life is rooted more deeply in Christ. The risen Jesus said: "Listen! I am standing at the door, knocking; if you hear my voice and open the door, I will come in to you and eat with you, and you with me" (Rev 3:20). Listen to the Word of God, open the door, and cross the threshold to an unimaginable dwelling with God!

SUGGESTIONS FOR INDIVIDUAL STUDY

• Make your Bible reading a time of prayer. Ask for God's guidance as you read the Scriptures.

• Try to study daily, or as often as possible according to the circumstances of your life.

• Read the Bible passage carefully, trying to understand both its meaning and its personal application as you read. Some persons find it helpful to read the passage aloud.

• Read the passage in another Bible translation. Each version adds to your understanding of the original text.

• Allow the commentary to help you comprehend and apply the scriptural text. The commentary is only a beginning, not the last word on the meaning of the passage.

• After reflecting on each question, write out your responses. The very act of writing will help you clarify your thoughts, bring new insights, and amplify your understanding.

• As you reflect on your answers, think about how you can live God's word in the context of your daily life.

• Conclude each daily lesson by reading the prayer and continuing with your own prayer from the heart.

• Make sure your reflections and prayers are matters of both the mind and the heart. A true encounter with God's word is always a transforming experience.

• Choose a word or a phrase from the lesson to carry with you throughout the day as a reminder of your encounter with God's life-changing word.

• Share your learning experience with at least one other person whom you trust for additional insights and affirmation. The ideal way to share learning is in a small group that meets regularly.

SUGGESTIONS FOR GROUP STUDY

• Meet regularly; weekly is ideal. Try to be on time and make attendance a high priority for the sake of the group. The average group meets for about an hour.

• Open each session with a prepared prayer, a song, or a reflection. Find some appropriate way to bring the group from the workaday world into a sacred time of graced sharing.

• If you have not been together before, name tags are very helpful as a group begins to become acquainted with the other group members.

• Spend the first session getting acquainted with one another, reading the Introduction aloud, and discussing the questions that follow.

• Appoint a group facilitator to provide guidance to the discussion. The role of facilitator may rotate among members each week. The facilitator simply keeps the discussion on track; each person shares responsibility for the group. There is no need for the facilitator to be a trained teacher.

• Try to study the six lessons on your own during the week. When you have done your own reflection and written your own answers, you will be better prepared to discuss the six scriptural lessons with the group. If you have not had an opportunity to study the passages during the week, meet with the group anyway to share support and insights.

• Participate in the discussion as much as you are able, offering your thoughts, insights, feelings, and decisions. You learn by sharing with others the fruits of your study.

• Be careful not to dominate the discussion. It is important that everyone in the group be offered an equal opportunity to share the results of their work. Try to link what you say to the comments of others so that the group remains on the topic.

• When discussing your own personal thoughts or feelings, use "I" language. Be as personal and honest as is appropriate and be very cautious about giving advice to others.

• Listen attentively to the other members of the group so as to learn from their insights. The words of the Bible affect each person in a different way, so a group provides a wealth of understanding for each member.

• Don't fear silence. Silence in a group is as important as silence in personal study. It allows individuals time to listen to the voice of God's Spirit and the opportunity to form their thoughts before they speak.

• Solicit several responses for each question. The thoughts of different people will build on the answers of others and will lead to deeper insights for all.

• Don't fear controversy. Differences of opinion are a sign of a healthy and honest group. If you cannot resolve an issue, continue on, agreeing to disagree. There is probably some truth in each viewpoint.

• Discuss the questions that seem most important for the group. There is no need to cover all the questions in the group session.

• Realize that some questions about the Bible cannot be resolved, even by experts. Don't get stuck on some issue for which there are no clear answers.

• Whatever is said in the group is said in confidence and should be regarded as such.

• Pray as a group in whatever way feels comfortable. Pray for the members of your group throughout the week.

Schedule for group study

Session 1: Introduction   Date _____

Session 2: Lessons 1-6   Date _____

Session 3: Lessons 7-12   Date _____

Session 4: Lessons 13-18   Date _____

Session 5: Lessons 19-24   Date _____

Session 6: Lessons 25-30   Date _____

At the name of Jesus every knee should bend, in heaven and on earth and under the earth, and every tongue should confess that Jesus Christ is Lord.
Phil 2:10–11

The Names of Jesus

Sometimes when we study the Bible, we get so caught up in the information it provides that we forget the purpose for our study. The essential purpose of reading the Scriptures is to know a person—Jesus Christ—more personally and more intimately. Paul expressed his intense desire to know Christ in his writings: "I regard everything as loss because of the surpassing value of knowing Christ Jesus my Lord" (Phil 3:8). Paul wanted to know Jesus more and more so that he could live more fully in Jesus.

There is a profound difference between "knowing about Jesus" and "knowing Jesus," just as there is a difference between watching a dance and entering the dance ourselves. We can read the Scriptures, read other books about Jesus, study for years, and even attain degrees in theology, and not really know Jesus. To know Jesus means to establish a personal relationship with him, to know him not just as a historical figure but "in person," as one who is real and alive, powerfully influencing our lives here and now.

Reflection and discussion

• What is involved in truly coming to know another person?

• What gives me a burning desire to know Jesus more personally?

What's in a Name?

In the ancient world in which the Bible was written, an essential aspect of knowing a person was to know the person's name. Knowing the name was far more personal than knowing information about the person; in fact, it was synonymous with knowing the person. When Moses wanted to know who God is, the book of Exodus recounts: "The Lord descended in the cloud and stood with him there, and proclaimed the name, The Lord" (Exod 34:5). "The Lord" in Hebrew is YHWH, a name that is hardly translatable, but is traditionally translated as "I am who I am."

Names in the ancient world of the Bible carry far more importance and value than they do today. Today we think of a name as a way to identify a person. In the Bible knowing someone's name, whether it be that of God or of a human being, allows a relationship to be established with that person. As the psalm proclaims: "Those who know your name put their trust in you" (Ps 9:10). Honoring and cherishing the name of God creates a personal and trusting bond with him.

Words in the biblical world have a vitality that is far greater than simply designating a person, place, or thing. God's naming other beings brings creation into existence: "He calls them all by name" (Isa 40:26). The words that form a person's name signify the very existence of that person. A person's name is kept in memory through posterity; to cut off a person's name means not only the death of the person, but the end of his or her existence. As the psalms declare: "You have blotted out their name for ever and ever" (Ps 9:5), and "May his name be blotted out in the second generation" (Ps 109:13; see also 1 Sam 24:21).

Reflection and discussion

• Why is it so wrong to misuse the name of God? How can I better honor and cherish the name of God?

• What is the meaning of my name? Does my name in any way characterize who I am?

The Power of Jesus' Name

The names of Jesus express his very nature and person. His names express and convey all of his saving deeds: "You were sanctified, you were justified in the name of the Lord Jesus Christ" (1 Cor 6:11). We participate in his saving power and authority when we act in his name. Peter healed in his name: "I have no silver or gold, but what I have I give you; in the name of Jesus Christ of Nazareth, stand up and walk" (Acts 3:6). The name of Jesus, the Nazorean, the Messiah, gave the crippled beggar something more than riches could purchase. James instructs the presbyters of the church to anoint the sick with oil "in the name of the Lord," and he states that the Lord will raise them up (Jam 5:14–15). When the church acts in the name of Jesus, he himself is at work in his ministers.

In his testimony before the Sanhedrin, Peter proclaimed the power of the name of Jesus. Peter was asked by the assembly, "By what power or by what name did you do this?" Peter answered them, "If we are questioned today because of a good deed done to someone who was sick and are asked how this man has been healed, let it be known to all of you, and to all the people of Israel, that this man is standing before you in good health by the name of Jesus Christ of Nazareth, whom you crucified, whom God raised from the dead. This Jesus is the stone that was rejected by you, the builders; it has become the cornerstone. There is salvation in no one else, for there is no other name under heaven given among mortals by which we must be saved" (Acts 4:7–12). Jesus is the expected Messiah, the Nazorean, the cornerstone of God's new temple. These names of Jesus convey his authority and power even when he is physically absent. When we speak or act in his name, he himself is at work among us.

The Bible is filled with a wide variety of names and titles of Jesus. We will reflect on thirty of these, each of which reveals something unique about who Jesus is. The more we reflect on these names, the better we will know him. As we call upon Jesus under his many names and titles, we will comprehend and experience more and more the fullness of who he is. Knowing Jesus better is reason enough to study his many names.

Yet, knowing Jesus is not the only reason for studying his names and titles. The better we know him, the better we will grasp the richness of his power at work within us. The more we know his names, the more we will be able to understand what he has done for us and what he can do for us today. We reflect on his marvelous names for this reason: every name that he bears is a blessing that he shares.

Reflection and discussion

• What are some of the names and titles of Jesus I have used in prayer?

• What does each of these names say about who Jesus desires to be in my life?

Honoring the Many Names of Jesus

No single name or title of Jesus can integrate the fullness of who he is. That is why biblical literature offers us a kaleidoscope of names. Each of them conveys one aspect of his person and power, yet none of them contains the fullness of who he is. The variety of these multifaceted names expresses the all-encompassing reality of Jesus.

Some of these names of Jesus originated with Jesus himself; others were crafted by the early church as they grew to understand Jesus more fully under the Spirit's guidance. Some of these names are unique to the New Testament writings; others have their origins in the Old Testament as names for God, Israel, or the Messiah.

Names such as the Nazorean, Carpenter, Messiah, the Son of Man, Prophet, and Rabbi most probably originated during the earthly ministry of Jesus. Titles such as the Word, the High Priest, King of Kings, and Alpha and Omega come from the early Church as they understood Jesus in the fullness of his risen glory.

Some names of Jesus are human images, such as Bridegroom, Shepherd, and Carpenter; others are images of transcendence, such as Word of God, Son of God, and Lord. Still other names express images of care and nourishment, such as Bread of Life, Living Water, Light of the World, and the True Vine.

Titles that are rooted in the Old Testament, such as Firstborn, Emmanuel, Prince of Peace, Son of David, Lamb, and Suffering Servant are given new significance when they are made names for Jesus. In the Old Testament, God is called the Shepherd, Light, Bridegroom, King, Lord, and I Am. As these images of God become titles for Jesus Christ, the New Testament is proclaiming that Jesus is the manifestation of God himself and that he shares in God's divinity.

The Old Testament imagery fulfilled in the names of Jesus is memorably summarized in the words of F. F. Bruce in *The New Testament Development of Old Testament Themes*: "In Jesus the promise is confirmed, the covenant is vindicated, salvation is brought near, sacred history has reached its climax, the perfect sacrifice has been offered and accepted, the great priest over the household of God has taken his seat at God's right hand, the Prophet like Moses has been raised up, the Son of David reigns, the kingdom of God has been inaugurated, the Son of Man has received dominion from the Ancient of Days, the Servant of the Lord, having been smitten to death for his people's transgression and borne the sin of many, has accomplished the divine purpose, has seen light after the travail of his soul, and is now exalted and extolled and made very high."

We honor the names of Jesus because he is our Lord, our Savior, our Messiah, our King. As Paul proclaimed in his New Testament hymn: "God highly exalted him and gave him the name that is above every name, so that at the name of Jesus every knee should bend, in heaven and on earth and under the earth, and every tongue should confess that Jesus Christ is Lord" (Phil 2:9–11). May we glorify and worship him as we ponder the mystery of his holy names.

Reflection and discussion

• What is the most difficult challenge I face as I begin this Bible study?

• What is my purpose for completing this Bible study?

Prayer

Lord Jesus Christ, you are called by manifold names throughout the Scriptures. I know there is healing, power, and grace in each of your holy names. As I study the many names you have been given during your earthly life and within the early Church, teach me about yourself. Help me to know you truly and personally. May all that I do be done in the name of the Father, and of the Son, and of the Holy Spirit. Amen.

SUGGESTIONS FOR FACILITATORS, GROUP SESSION 1

1. If the group is meeting for the first time, or if there are newcomers joining the group, it is helpful to provide nametags.

2. Ask the participants to introduce themselves and tell the group a bit about themselves. Ask one or more of these introductory questions:
   • What drew you to join this group?
   • What is your biggest fear in beginning this Bible study?
   • How is beginning this study like a "threshold" for you?

3. Distribute the books to the members of the group.

4. Invite the participants to join in this prayer:
Come upon us, Holy Spirit, to enlighten and guide us as we begin this study of the names of Jesus. You inspired the biblical authors to express the wonders of the person of Jesus in many ways through different names. Now stir our minds and our hearts to understand these names of Jesus and to proclaim their truth for others. Motivate us to read the Scriptures, give us a love for God's word, and help us to know Jesus more personally and more richly. Bless us during this session and throughout the coming week with the fire of your love.

5. Read the Introduction aloud, pausing at each question for discussion. Group members may wish to write the insights of the group as each question is discussed. Encourage several members of the group to respond to each question.

6. Don't feel compelled to finish the complete Introduction during the session. It is better to allow sufficient time to talk about the questions raised than to rush to the end. Group members may read any remaining sections on their own after the group meeting.

7. Instruct group members to read the first six lessons on their own during the six days before the next group meeting. They should write out their own answers to the questions as preparation for next week's group discussion.

8. Fill in the date for each group meeting under "Schedule for Group Study."

9. Conclude by praying aloud together the prayer at the end of the Introduction.

"You are to name him Jesus, for he will save his people from their sins."
Matt 1:21

Jesus

MATTHEW 1:18–25 ¹⁸*Now the birth of Jesus the Messiah took place in this way. When his mother Mary had been engaged to Joseph, but before they lived together, she was found to be with child from the Holy Spirit.* ¹⁹*Her husband Joseph, being a righteous man and unwilling to expose her to public disgrace, planned to dismiss her quietly.* ²⁰*But just when he had resolved to do this, an angel of the Lord appeared to him in a dream and said, "Joseph, son of David, do not be afraid to take Mary as your wife, for the child conceived in her is from the Holy Spirit.* ²¹*She will bear a son, and you are to name him Jesus, for he will save his people from their sins."* ²²*All this took place to fulfill what had been spoken by the Lord through the prophet:*

²³*"Look, the virgin shall conceive and bear a son,*
and they shall name him Emmanuel,"

which means, "God is with us." ²⁴*When Joseph awoke from sleep, he did as the angel of the Lord commanded him; he took her as his wife,* ²⁵*but had no marital relations with her until she had borne a son; and he named him Jesus.*

LUKE 1:26–31 ²⁶*In the sixth month the angel Gabriel was sent by God to a town in Galilee called Nazareth,* ²⁷*to a virgin engaged to a man whose name was Joseph, of the house of David. The virgin's name was Mary.* ²⁸*And he came to her* *and said, "Greetings, favored one! The Lord is with you." ²⁹But she was much* *perplexed by his words and pondered what sort of greeting this might be. ³⁰The* *angel said to her, "Do not be afraid, Mary, for you have found favor with God.* *³¹And now, you will conceive in your womb and bear a son, and you will name* *him Jesus."*

In ancient Israel, most people had only one name, the name we think of as a first name or given name. Jesus in English is from the Hebrew name *Yeshua*. We see this name more commonly written as Joshua. The name was written in the Greek translation as *Iesous*, from which we get Jesus.

The name Jesus literally means "Yahweh saves." The name was common among Jews two thousand years ago, but only Jesus from Nazareth embodied the full sense of this name by saving God's people from their worst enemies. The name was a promise and foreshadowing of the work Jesus would accomplish.

The name Jesus was divinely chosen and revealed to Joseph and Mary before his birth. In the revelation of his conception to both Joseph and Mary, the angel proclaimed that his name was to be Jesus (Matt 1:21; Luke 1:31). In Matthew's account, the angel adds, "for he will save his people from their sins." Salvation can only be accomplished by one sent to do the work of God.

Because his name was given by God, Jesus' name connects his life with God's saving plan made known throughout the Hebrew Scriptures. In the Old Testament, Joshua brought the people of Israel into the Promised Land. Joshua led them in battle to defeat their enemies and claim their inheritance. Before his death, Joshua proclaimed: "All the good things that the Lord your God promised concerning you have been fulfilled for you" (Josh 23:15). Yet Jesus, the new Joshua, will fulfill God's promises in ways never before imagined by the Israelites of old. In him, God will save all people and bring them into the promised inheritance of God's kingdom.

In the name of Jesus, his disciples healed (Acts 3:6); in the name of Jesus, his disciples preached and taught (Acts 4:18). They proclaimed that "there is no other name under heaven given among mortals by which we must be saved" (Acts 4:12). Today, when the name of Jesus is often used irreverently, let us recall the words of an early Christian hymn: "God gave him the name that is above every name, so that at the name of Jesus every knee should bend, in heaven and on earth and under the earth, and every tongue should confess that Jesus Christ is Lord" (Phil 2:9–11).

Reflection and discussion

• What or who are my greatest enemies from which I need God's rescue?

• Do I trust that Jesus can save me from all that hinders me from eternal life?

• How can I live my life more fully "in the name of Jesus"?

Prayer

Jesus, you did not come to condemn but to save the world. Help me live as one being saved from sin, fear, death, and a meaningless life. Let me call upon your name with a joyful confidence.

**What had been spoken through the prophets might be fulfilled.
"He will be called a Nazorean."** Matt 2:23

The Nazorean

MATTHEW 2:19–23 ¹⁹*When Herod died, an angel of the Lord suddenly appeared in a dream to Joseph in Egypt and said,* ²⁰*"Get up, take the child and his mother, and go to the land of Israel, for those who were seeking the child's life are dead."* ²¹*Then Joseph got up, took the child and his mother, and went to the land of Israel.* ²²*But when he heard that Archelaus was ruling over Judea in place of his father Herod, he was afraid to go there. And after being warned in a dream, he went away to the district of Galilee.* ²³*There he made his home in a town called Nazareth, so that what had been spoken through the prophets might be fulfilled, "He will be called a Nazorean."*

MATTHEW 26:69–72 ⁶⁹*Now Peter was sitting outside in the courtyard. A servant-girl came to him and said, "You also were with Jesus the Galilean."* ⁷⁰*But he denied it before all of them, saying, "I do not know what you are talking about."* ⁷¹*When he went out to the porch, another servant-girl saw him, and she said to the bystanders, "This man was with Jesus of Nazareth."* ⁷²*Again he denied it with an oath, "I do not know the man."*

Probably the most common names used to identify our Lord when he walked the earth were "Jesus of Nazareth" or "Jesus the Nazorean." Though he was born in Bethlehem of Judea, Jesus was identified with the town in which he grew up, Nazareth in Galilee.

The hillside village of Nazareth was small and obscure in the days of Jesus. Unlike the larger cities of Galilee and Judea, Nazareth was totally unspectacular. Upon first hearing about Jesus, Nathanael exclaimed, "Can anything good come out of Nazareth?" (John 1:46). It was not the kind of place where a strict Jew would want to live, for it had no significance in Israel's religious tradition. Its simple inhabitants even spoke Aramaic with a rough accent (Matt 26:73). The early Christians were derisively referred to as the "sect of the Nazoreans" (Acts 24:5). Jesus identified himself with the insignificant and rejected people of his day, even with the people of Nazareth.

Matthew's gospel adds further significance to the name Nazorean by stating that "He will be called a Nazorean" was a fulfillment of the prophets (Matt 2:23). Yet no explicit prophecy in the Old Testament resembles this text. In fact, no text in the Hebrew Scriptures mentions Nazareth. Probably Matthew was recalling Old Testament texts whose words were similar to Nazareth. Isaiah 11:1 proclaims that the future Davidic king would be a *netser* (a branch or shoot) from the roots of Jesse. Judges 13:5 and 7 speak of Samson, the future deliverer of Israel, as a *nazir*, one who is consecrated to God. Thus Matthew may be saying that Jesus was simultaneously from Nazareth and also the one consecrated by God to be that expected branch from David's line.

Nazareth, though an obscure town, is nevertheless part of God's plan for manifesting the Nazorean to the world. Jesus became known and loved as the man from Nazareth. The presence of the Nazorean was a source of hope for the people he touched. The blind man began to shout when he was told, "Jesus of Nazareth is passing by" (Luke 18:37). Yet, one of his closest followers proclaimed "I do not know the man" when a maid said, "This man was with Jesus of Nazareth" (Matt 26:71–72).

Jesus was never trendy or chic. He befriended the poor, the sick, the prostitutes and thieves. Everyone who has ever felt outcast can find a companion in Jesus of Nazareth.

Reflection and discussion

• How may people know that I am a disciple of Jesus of Nazareth?

• Do I identify myself with the insignificant and outcast ones, or do I deny my association with those rejected from more "proper" society?

• In what way is my identity partly determined by the city and town of my origin?

Prayer

Jesus of Nazareth, you were rejected by many, yet you are the source of healing for all. Heal my blindness and my prejudices, so that I may acknowledge you and befriend the outcasts. Teach me to proudly acknowledge that I am your disciple.

"**Is not this the carpenter, the son of Mary?**" Mark 6:3

The Carpenter

MARK 6:1–6 ¹*He left that place and came to his hometown, and his disciples followed him.* ²*On the sabbath he began to teach in the synagogue, and many who heard him were astounded. They said, "Where did this man get all this? What is this wisdom that has been given to him? What deeds of power are being done by his hands!* ³*Is not this the carpenter, the son of Mary and brother of James and Joses and Judas and Simon, and are not his sisters here with us?" And they took offense at him.* ⁴*Then Jesus said to them, "Prophets are not without honor, except in their hometown, and among their own kin, and in their own house."* ⁵*And he could do no deed of power there, except that he laid his hands on a few sick people and cured them.* ⁶*And he was amazed at their unbelief.*

MATTHEW 13:54–58 ⁵⁴*He came to his hometown and began to teach the people in their synagogue, so that they were astounded and said, "Where did this man get this wisdom and these deeds of power?* ⁵⁵*Is not this the carpenter's son? Is not his mother called Mary? And are not his brothers James and Joseph and Simon and Judas?* ⁵⁶*And are not all his sisters with us? Where then did this man get all this?"* ⁵⁷*And they took offense at him. But Jesus said to them, "Prophets are not without honor except in their own country and in their own house."* ⁵⁸*And he did not do many deeds of power there, because of their unbelief.*

Jesus is called a carpenter (Mark 6:3) and the son of a carpenter (Matt 13:55). The Greek word used is *tekton*, a word designating a craftsman who shapes wood, metal, or stone. Jesus was not a carpenter in the sense in which we use the word today—one who works exclusively with wood. Since wood was relatively rare and was often imported in the Palestine of Jesus' day, a skilled builder would have worked primarily with stone, probably also with wood and metal.

The carpenters mentioned in the Old Testament built agricultural tools and constructed houses. David hired carpenters from Phoenicia to build his palace with imported cedars (2 Sam 5:11). After the exile, carpenters returned to Jerusalem and helped to rebuild the Temple (Ezra 3:7). Isaiah depicts a carpenter as one who stretched a line, marked it with a stylus, shaped wood with a plane, and measured it with a compass (Isa 44:13).

In Nazareth, Jesus was born into the home of Joseph the carpenter. Joseph taught Jesus his trade and he taught him to experience the dignity and humility of honest labor. Later rabbis taught: "If you do not teach your son to work, you teach him how to steal." The Jewish people taught their children to work their own trades: as fishermen, farmers, tentmakers, and carpenters. Work was a holy task, a sacred responsibility. Like all Jews, Jesus worked hard six days of the week; but on the seventh, he honored the Sabbath and rested from his labor (Exod 20:8–10). Jesus spent his early years building and repairing the homes and tools of his village. His years of labor helped him understand the burdens and needs of the people who came to him.

During his public life, Jesus applied his vocation as a carpenter to the work of building the church (Matt 16:18). We are the living stones which he is using to build a holy temple to God (1 Pet 2:5). Like a good craftsman who sees the potential in a piece of wood or stone, Jesus sees what we can be. He forms us into something useful and beautiful. The divine carpenter continues to build, shape, and repair us. And he will see his work through to its completion.

Reflection and discussion

• Am I ready to be sawed, planed, sanded, or polished by the great carpenter?

• Do I see the work I do each day as an honorable calling given to me by God?

• Do I do my best in all that I do? How can I change so that my work gives greater honor to God?

Prayer

Jesus, you learned the skills of a carpenter in Nazareth. Teach me the dignity of human work and to honor the tasks of all laborers. Help me as I work this day, so that all I do may be for the glory of God and contribute to the betterment of the world you have given me.

"Who do you say that I am?" Peter answered him, "You are the Messiah."
Mark 8:29

The Messiah

MARK 8:27–30 *²⁷Jesus went on with his disciples to the villages of Caesarea Philippi; and on the way he asked his disciples, "Who do people say that I am?" ²⁸And they answered him, "John the Baptist; and others, Elijah; and still others, one of the prophets." ²⁹He asked them, "But who do you say that I am?" Peter answered him, "You are the Messiah." ³⁰And he sternly ordered them not to tell anyone about him.*

MARK 14:60–65 *⁶⁰Then the high priest stood up before them and asked Jesus, "Have you no answer? What is it that they testify against you?" ⁶¹But he was silent and did not answer. Again the high priest asked him, "Are you the Messiah, the Son of the Blessed One?" ⁶²Jesus said, "I am; and 'you will see the Son of Man seated at the right hand of the Power,' and 'coming with the clouds of heaven.'"*

⁶³Then the high priest tore his clothes and said, "Why do we still need witnesses? ⁶⁴You have heard his blasphemy! What is your decision?" All of them condemned him as deserving death. ⁶⁵Some began to spit on him, to blindfold him, and to strike him, saying to him, "Prophesy!" The guards also took him over and beat him.

Jesus demonstrated by his miracles, his teachings, and in many other convincing ways that he was the Messiah of the Old Testament prophecies, yet he was not the kind of Messiah expected by most of the Jews of his time. They looked to the coming Messiah to lead their armies against the hated Roman overlord, and to establish a mighty empire with its capital at Jerusalem. Jesus never rejected the name Messiah, but he clearly did not proclaim that title for himself because of its associations with worldly rule. In fact, even though many would come to recognize Jesus as the Messiah, the gospels indicate that Jesus did not want to be proclaimed as the Messiah until the end of his life (Mark 8:30). He continually refused to display his power for show or to rouse the masses. Clearly, in Mark's gospel, Jesus had a nobler, grander, and more spiritual goal for his messianic reign.

When Jesus asked the critical question, "Who do you say that I am?" Peter answered correctly: "You are the Messiah." But Peter's inability to understand that Jesus must be rejected and suffer death indicates Peter's inability to understand the true nature of Jesus' mission as the Messiah. At his trial before the high priest, Jesus acknowledged that he is the Messiah, after which Jesus was accused of blasphemy and condemned to death. His messianic kingdom would be established through humility, suffering, and death.

The Hebrew word for messiah simply meant "anointed" and in the Old Testament it referred to one who was ceremonially anointed with oil for a sacred mission. Prophets, priests, and kings were anointed with the oil of the olive for the offices in which they served. Because their missions were temporary and failed to fulfill the hopes expressed in Scripture, Israel increasingly anticipated the coming of the Anointed One, the Messiah, who would truly fulfill the scriptural expectations about the messianic kingdom.

The New Testament proclaims that Jesus is the Messiah, or in Greek, the *Christos* (Christ). He was anointed not by human hands but by God, not with olive oil but with the Holy Spirit. Thus Jesus could testify about himself, "The Spirit of the Lord is upon me, because the Lord has anointed me" (Luke 4:18).

Jesus is commonly called "the Christ;" often he is designated as Jesus Christ. The name of Christ indicates that Jesus of Nazareth is the expected one of Israel, the one who has perfectly fulfilled the hopes expressed in the ancient Scriptures. As Christians, we proclaim ourselves as followers of this Christ, the Messiah of God.

Reflection and discussion

• Why did Jesus refuse the title of Messiah during his earthly ministry?

• How would I answer the question posed to Peter by Jesus: "Who do you say that I am?"

• What are the daily implications of calling myself a Christian, a follower of the Anointed One?

Prayer

Jesus, Messiah of Israel and fulfillment of my hopes, help me trust in your power. You are the humble and suffering Messiah; help me follow the way of your cross to my promised inheritance.

"Rabbi, we know that you are a teacher who has come from God." John 3:2

Rabbi

JOHN 1:37–39 *37 The two disciples heard him say this, and they followed Jesus. 38 When Jesus turned and saw them following, he said to them, "What are you looking for?" They said to him, "Rabbi" (which translated means Teacher), "where are you staying?" 39 He said to them, "Come and see." They came and saw where he was staying, and they remained with him that day. It was about four o'clock in the afternoon.*

JOHN 3:1–5 *1 Now there was a Pharisee named Nicodemus, a leader of the Jews. 2 He came to Jesus by night and said to him, "Rabbi, we know that you are a teacher who has come from God; for no one can do these signs that you do apart from the presence of God." 3 Jesus answered him, "Very truly, I tell you, no one can see the kingdom of God without being born from above." 4 Nicodemus said to him, "How can anyone be born after having grown old? Can one enter a second time into the mother's womb and be born?" 5 Jesus answered, "Very truly, I tell you, no one can enter the kingdom of God without being born of water and Spirit."*

J esus is frequently addressed as rabbi in the gospels. The Hebrew term *rab* designated a person of high rank and is translated as "great one," "master," or "chief." By the time the gospel of John was written, the title rabbi ("my master") had become a title of respect given by students and seekers after knowledge to their teachers. Since Jesus gathered disciples, taught in the synagogues, and debated his opponents, it is not surprising that he was addressed as "rabbi" in the gospels.

In John's gospel, Jesus is first addressed as rabbi by two disciples of John the Baptist after Jesus asked them, "What are you looking for?" John translates the Hebrew term *rabbi* for his Greek audience as "Teacher" (John 1:38). The disciples respond with another question: "Where are you staying?" Jesus answers with an invitation: "Come and see" (John 1:39). "Staying with Jesus" and "coming to see" are both indications of developing faith in the gospel of John.

Nicodemus, a leader among the Jews, came to Jesus at night and addressed him as rabbi. He acknowledged that Jesus is "a teacher who has come from God" (John 3:2). Their dialogue indicates Jesus' skilled use of language for teaching. He says that no one can see the kingdom of God without being "born from above" (John 3:3). The words Jesus uses can also mean "born anew." Nicodemus opens the dialogue by assuming the most literal meaning: a person would have to come forth from the womb again. But Jesus teaches that the Spirit is the agent of this "rebirth" that occurs when one enters God's kingdom.

At the resurrection, Mary Magdalene recognized the risen Jesus and called him *Rabbouni*, another form of the title of rabbi (John 20:16). Like Mary and the other disciples, we are invited to continue to listen to and follow Jesus, who reveals himself as the master teacher.

Reflection and discussion

• What is the greatest thing Jesus has taught me?

• How does the dialogue of Jesus with Nicodemus indicate his teaching skills?

• What particular characteristics and abilities did Jesus possess that all teachers could learn to imitate?

• What is the evidence that I have been reborn in God's Spirit?

Prayer

My Teacher and Master, I want to follow you, to learn from you, and to dwell with you. Help me recognize your risen presence and experience new birth in your Holy Spirit.

Two blind men followed Jesus, crying loudly,
"Have mercy on us, Son of David!" Matt 9:27

Son of David

MATTHEW 9:27–31 *27As Jesus went on from there, two blind men followed him, crying loudly, "Have mercy on us, Son of David!" 28When he entered the house, the blind men came to him; and Jesus said to them, "Do you believe that I am able to do this?" They said to him, "Yes, Lord." 29Then he touched their eyes and said, "According to your faith let it be done to you." 30And their eyes were opened. Then Jesus sternly ordered them, "See that no one knows of this." 31But they went away and spread the news about him throughout that district.*

MATTHEW 22:41–46 *41Now while the Pharisees were gathered together, Jesus asked them this question: 42 "What do you think of the Messiah? Whose son is he?" They said to him, "The son of David." 43He said to them, "How is it then that David by the Spirit calls him Lord, saying, 44 'The Lord said to my Lord, Sit at my right hand, until I put your enemies under your feet'"?*

45If David thus calls him Lord, how can he be his son?" 46No one was able to give him an answer, nor from that day did anyone dare to ask him any more questions.

D avid, a simple shepherd from Bethlehem, became the great king of Israel. Jesus, a descendant of David through his father Joseph, is called the Son of David throughout the gospels, beginning with the genealogy of both Matthew and Luke. Matthew began his gospel by tracing the ancestry of Jesus from Abraham, through the royal line of King David (1:1). In Luke's annunciation account, the angel proclaims that "the Lord God will give to him the throne of his ancestor David" (Luke 1:32). Paul, too, declares that Jesus "descended from David according to the flesh" (Rom 1:3).

An ancient prophecy promised David that his descendants would always rule over Israel (2 Sam 7:16). Psalm 89 declares, "I will establish his line for ever, and his throne as long as the heavens endure" (Ps 89:29). Although the political power of the house of David was eventually shattered, God's promise of an eternal dynasty of David endured and the Jews longed for a new king from the line of David. God's promise was ultimately fulfilled in the coming of Jesus. His kingly rule would outlast time itself.

In the gospel of Matthew, Jesus is proclaimed as Son of David, particularly in association with his healing miracles. The prophet Isaiah had declared that the blind, the deaf, the lame, and the mute would be healed in the glorious age to come: "Then the eyes of the blind shall be opened, and the ears of the deaf unstopped; then the lame shall leap like a deer, and the tongue of the speechless sing for joy" (Isa 35:5–6). Those calling on Jesus as Son of David were professing their trust that Jesus is the king they were waiting for (Matt 9:27; 12:23; 15:22; 20:30–31). The ministry of the Son of David leads up to his entry into Jerusalem, when the crowds sing out: "Hosanna to the Son of David! Blessed is the one who comes in the name of the Lord!" (21:9, 15).

While debating with the Pharisees, Jesus confirms the Jewish expectation that the Messiah would be the Son of David (Matt 22:42). But he challenges their easy assumptions by quoting from a psalm of David, who calls the Messiah "my lord." If David calls him Lord, then the Messiah must be greater than simply a descendant of David (22:44–45). He is not only the son of David, but also the Son of God.

Reflection and discussion

• For what infirmities do I need the healing help of the Son of David?

• What enemies must be subdued in order for Christ to reign as king over my life?

• Why is the royal rule of Jesus so difficult to recognize in the Church and in the world?

Prayer

Hosanna to the Son of David! Blessed is the one who comes in the name of the Lord! Son of David, have mercy on me. Heal me of my faults and weaknesses, and help me acknowledge you as king over my life.

SUGGESTIONS FOR FACILITATORS, GROUP SESSION 2

1. If there are newcomers who were not present for the first group session, introduce them now.

2. You may want to pray this prayer as a group:

Jesus, at the sound of your precious name, every knee should bend, in heaven and on earth. The names you were given on earth are powerful reminders of who you are: Nazorean, Carpenter, Messiah, Rabbi, and Son of David. We want to know you better and more deeply. Teach us the meaning of each of your many names. We want to be able to answer for ourselves the question that you posed to Peter: "Who do you say that I am?" As we gather as your disciples, encourage us to listen to God's word, allow it to penetrate our hearts, and give us the confidence necessary to put it into practice in our daily lives. Bless us with your Holy Spirit as we learn about you together.

3. Ask one or more of the following questions:
   - What was your biggest challenge in Bible study over this past week?
   - What did you learn about Jesus from your study this week?
   - What did you learn about yourself this week?

4. Discuss lessons 1 through 6 together. Assuming that group members have read the Scripture and commentary during the week, there is no need to read it aloud. As you review each lesson, you might want to briefly summarize the Scripture passages of each lesson and ask the group what stands out most clearly about the name of Jesus in the reading.

5. Choose one or more of the questions for reflection and discussion from each lesson to talk over as a group. You may want to ask group members which question was most challenging or helpful to them as you review each lesson.

6. Keep the discussion moving, but don't rush the discussion in order to complete more questions. Allow time for the questions that provoke the most discussion.

7. Instruct group members to complete lessons 7 through 12 on their own during the six days before the next group meeting. They should write out their own answers to the questions as preparation for next week's group discussion.

8. Conclude by praying aloud together the prayer at the end of lesson 6, or any other prayer you choose.

Then they will see "the Son of Man coming in clouds" with great power and glory. Mark 13:26

Son of Man

MARK 8:31–38 *³¹Then he began to teach them that the Son of Man must undergo great suffering, and be rejected by the elders, the chief priests, and the scribes, and be killed, and after three days rise again. ³²He said all this quite openly. And Peter took him aside and began to rebuke him. ³³But turning and looking at his disciples, he rebuked Peter and said, "Get behind me, Satan! For you are setting your mind not on divine things but on human things."*

³⁴He called the crowd with his disciples, and said to them, "If any want to become my followers, let them deny themselves and take up their cross and follow me. ³⁵For those who want to save their life will lose it, and those who lose their life for my sake, and for the sake of the gospel, will save it. ³⁶For what will it profit them to gain the whole world and forfeit their life? ³⁷Indeed, what can they give in return for their life? ³⁸Those who are ashamed of me and of my words in this adulterous and sinful generation, of them the Son of Man will also be ashamed when he comes in the glory of his Father with the holy angels."

MARK 13:24–27 *²⁴"But in those days, after that suffering, the sun will be darkened, and the moon will not give its light, ²⁵and the stars will be falling from heaven, and the powers in the heavens will be shaken. ²⁶Then they will see "the Son of Man coming in clouds" with great power and glory. ²⁷Then he*

will send out the angels, and gather his elect from the four winds, from the
ends of the earth to the ends of heaven.

The title Son of Man occurs only on the lips of Jesus himself in the gospels. It is the designation Jesus used most often for himself. He used the title in three main contexts: when describing his earthly ministry, when predicting his suffering and death, and when anticipating his future return and reign upon the earth.

The phrase Son of Man was used frequently in the Old Testament to refer to an individual human being, in contrast to God or an angel. Jesus used the term during his earthly life to express his human nature. As Son of Man, Jesus is subject to frailty, weakness, pain, and mortality. In each of his passion predictions, Jesus refers to himself as the Son of Man who must undergo great suffering, rejection, and death (Mark 8:31; 9:31; 10:33–34).

Another use of the term in the Old Testament has extraordinary implications for its usage in the gospels. Daniel 7 describes a vision of "a son of man coming with the clouds of heaven." He receives "dominion and glory and kingship" from God, and his royal reign is everlasting (Dan 7:13–14). The heavenly figure seems nearly equivalent to God in power and authority. When calling himself the Son of Man in the gospels, Jesus also referred to this royal vision to describe himself as the one through whom the salvation of God's people will be realized.

The authority of Jesus as Son of Man is gradually revealed. Jesus refers to himself as Son of Man when expressing his divine prerogative: "The Son of Man has authority on earth to forgive sins" (Mark 2:10); "The Son of Man is lord even of the sabbath" (Mark 2:28). Then Jesus uses this title to foretell his role as the future exalted judge. In teaching his disciples about his future coming (Mark 8:38; 13:26) and in responding to the high priest at his trial (Mark 14:62), Jesus said that the Son of Man would come in the clouds, bearing his Father's glory and power and accompanied by the angels.

The authority of Jesus is not based on dominating power, but it is achieved through suffering. He is like a king who lays down his crown and scepter in order to live among his subjects as one of them. He took the unlikely path through suffering to exaltation. He teaches us that our own exaltation must come through self-emptying and suffering with him. Jesus became Son of Man so that we can become children of God, if, as Paul says, "we suffer with him so that we may also be glorified with him" (Rom 8:17).

Reflection and discussion

• Why did Jesus become human rather than coming to us in divine glory?

• Do I anticipate the day that Jesus will come again in glory? How do I keep watchful and expectant?

• What can I do now to prepare for the reign of Christ upon the earth?

Prayer

Jesus, Son of Man, thank you for coming to this world as a man so that I can see God's presence within my own humanity. I long for the day when you will come in glory to bring the fullness of your Father's kingdom.

He is the beginning, the firstborn from the dead. Col 1:18

Firstborn

COLOSSIANS 1:15–18 [15]*He is the image of the invisible God, the firstborn of all creation;* [16]*for in him all things in heaven and on earth were created, things visible and invisible, whether thrones or dominions or rulers or powers—all things have been created through him and for him.* [17]*He himself is before all things, and in him all things hold together.* [18]*He is the head of the body, the church; he is the beginning, the firstborn from the dead, so that he might come to have first place in everything.*

ROMANS 8:28–30 [28]*We know that all things work together for good for those who love God, who are called according to his purpose.* [29]*For those whom he foreknew he also predestined to be conformed to the image of his Son, in order that he might be the firstborn within a large family.* [30]*And those whom he predestined he also called; and those whom he called he also justified; and those whom he justified he also glorified.*

Jesus was the "firstborn" son of Mary (Luke 2:7), an important position in a Jewish family. The firstborn was to be consecrated to God (Exod 13:2; Luke 2:23) and receive a double share of the inheritance as the birthright (Deut 21:15–17). Sometimes the rights of the firstborn were given to one who was not born first, as in the lives of Isaac and Jacob. King David was not Jesse's firstborn, but he was made God's firstborn, the highest of all the world's kings (Ps 89:27). In Exodus, we see that God designated Israel as his own firstborn: "Thus says the Lord: Israel is my firstborn son" (Exod 4:22). Thus the designation "firstborn" expresses priority, superiority, and dignity.

The New Testament writings name Jesus as the "firstborn" in several senses. Not only is Jesus the firstborn of Mary; he is called the firstborn of God (Heb 1:6). In Paul's writings, he is called the "firstborn of all creation" (Col 1:15); that is, he is superior to everything in creation and he existed prior to everything in creation, for "all things have been created through him and for him" (Col 1:16). "All things" includes those in heaven and on earth, things visible and invisible. Creation is what God has made to glorify and serve his firstborn. God charges us, then, as stewards to care for the created world so that it may give glory to Christ.

Jesus is also "firstborn from the dead" (Col 1:18; Rev 1:5). This does not mean that he was the first person ever to come back to earthly life; many in the Old Testament and the gospels were raised after their death. But Christ is the firstborn of the dead into eternal life, blazing a trail for us to his Father (see 1 Cor 15:20–24).

Finally, Jesus is "the firstborn within a large family" (Rom 8:29). We are all brothers and sisters within the family of God—a family in which Christ is the firstborn. One day we will be like him and share in his home forever. He has inherited everything from the Father, but he shares his inheritance with us all. The book of Hebrews calls the heavenly Jerusalem "the assembly of the firstborn" (Heb 12:23). We are destined to share forever in all the love and blessings that the Father has given to the Son.

Reflection and discussion

• What motivation does the letter to the Colossians offer me to care for creation?

• Do I fear or look forward to the day when Christ will raise me from death?

• What is the inheritance that Jesus will share with me in his Father's house?

Prayer

Jesus, you are firstborn of Mary and firstborn of a whole assembly of brothers and sisters. Thank you for inviting me into your family and for sharing your inheritance with me. Help me to care for what I have been given on earth and to look forward to my inheritance in heaven.

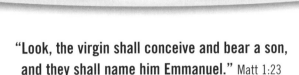

"Look, the virgin shall conceive and bear a son,
and they shall name him Emmanuel." Matt 1:23

Emmanuel

MATTHEW 1:18–25 ¹⁸*Now the birth of Jesus the Messiah took place in this way. When his mother Mary had been engaged to Joseph, but before they lived together, she was found to be with child from the Holy Spirit.* ¹⁹*Her husband Joseph, being a righteous man and unwilling to expose her to public disgrace, planned to dismiss her quietly.* ²⁰*But just when he had resolved to do this, an angel of the Lord appeared to him in a dream and said, "Joseph, son of David, do not be afraid to take Mary as your wife, for the child conceived in her is from the Holy Spirit.* ²¹*She will bear a son, and you are to name him Jesus, for he will save his people from their sins."* ²²*All this took place to fulfill what had been spoken by the Lord through the prophet:* ²³*"Look, the virgin shall conceive and bear a son, and they shall name him Emmanuel," which means, "God is with us."* ²⁴*When Joseph awoke from sleep, he did as the angel of the Lord commanded him; he took her as his wife,* ²⁵*but had no marital relations with her until she had borne a son; and he named him Jesus.*

MATTHEW 28:16–20 ¹⁶*Now the eleven disciples went to Galilee, to the mountain to which Jesus had directed them.* ¹⁷*When they saw him, they worshiped him; but some doubted.* ¹⁸*And Jesus came and said to them, "All authority in heaven and on earth has been given to me.* ¹⁹*Go therefore and make disci-*

ples of all nations, baptizing them in the name of the Father and of the Son and of the Holy Spirit, [20] and teaching them to obey everything that I have command-ed you. And remember, I am with you always, to the end of the age."

The name Emmanuel means "God is with us" (Matt 1:23). The Old Testament verse proclaiming the coming of Emmanuel is cited by Matthew from Isaiah 7:14. The Emmanuel prophecy was an oracle of hope given originally to the house of David in the eighth century before Christ. It referred to the coming birth of a king, one who would restore the glorious line of David and be a sign that God was with Israel. Since the kings of Judah never fulfilled the high ideals of the Emmanuel prophecies (espe-cially Isaiah 7, 9, and 11), the expectation of a future, ideal messianic king grew stronger. Though the ancient prophet could not have known the full meaning of his words in the divine plan, the inspired evangelists and the early Christians were able to recognize these texts as expressing God's plan for the coming of Jesus.

This text from Isaiah 7:14 expresses and fortifies the early community's faith in the messianic identity of Jesus and his virginal conception. Though the Hebrew text calls the woman "a maiden," the Greek text of Isaiah, the text more familiar to the early Christians, calls the woman "the virgin." Thus, her child is clearly the firstborn. Through this Emmanuel prophecy, Matthew's gospel proclaims that Jesus is the long-awaited Savior, that he was born of the Virgin Mary, and that in him God is with his people in a completely new way.

The name Emmanuel, "God is with us," completes the divine promise made to the patriarchs and prophets throughout the Old Testament: "I will be with you." Because Jesus saves his people from the great divide of sin, God's people are able to recognize the divine presence in Jesus. The Emmanuel of Matthew's first chapter anticipates the end of his gospel when Jesus proclaims, "I am with you always" (Matthew 28:20).

There may be people we have loved whom we are missing today because of distance, departure, divorce, or death. The pain of separation in human life is very real and agonizing. Yet, there is one utterly dependable person in whom we can trust. He has promised, "I will never leave you or forsake you" (Joshua 1:5; Hebrews 13:5). We can depend upon him always; he is Emmanuel, God with us always.

Reflection and discussion

• Do I believe that God is with me in the pains and struggles of life as well as the joys and successes?

• Who am I missing today? How do the promises of Jesus to be with us always give me hope?

• Do I trust that Jesus will be with me through my own personal death and into eternity?

Prayer

Jesus, Emmanuel, you are not a God who is distant and unconcerned, but one who shares the experiences of my life. Be with me when I wake up and when I fall asleep, when I win and when I fail, when I die and when I rise.

He is named **Wonderful Counsellor, Mighty God, Everlasting Father, Prince of Peace.** Isa 9:6

Prince of Peace

ISAIAH 9:1–6 ¹*But there will be no gloom for those who were in anguish. In the former time he brought into contempt the land of Zebulun and the land of Naphtali, but in the latter time he will make glorious the way of the sea, the land beyond the Jordan, Galilee of the nations.*

²*The people who walked in darkness*
  have seen a great light;
those who lived in a land of deep darkness—
  on them light has shined.
³*You have multiplied the nation,*
  you have increased its joy;
they rejoice before you
  as with joy at the harvest,
  as people exult when dividing plunder.
⁴*For the yoke of their burden,*
  and the bar across their shoulders,
  the rod of their oppressor,
  you have broken as on the day of Midian.
⁵*For all the boots of the tramping warriors*
  and all the garments rolled in blood

shall be burned as fuel for the fire.
⁶*For a child has been born for us,*
  a son given to us;
authority rests upon his shoulders;
  and he is named
Wonderful Counsellor, Mighty God,
  Everlasting Father, Prince of Peace.

JOHN 14:25–27
²⁵*"I have said these things to you while I am still with you.* ²⁶*But the Advocate, the Holy Spirit, whom the Father will send in my name, will teach you everything, and remind you of all that I have said to you.* ²⁷*Peace I leave with you; my peace I give to you. I do not give to you as the world gives. Do not let your hearts be troubled, and do not let them be afraid."*

Isaiah proclaimed that the future messianic king would be called Prince of Peace. When the Prince is on his throne, the promises of peace found in the prophets will be fulfilled. The wolf and the lamb, the lion and the calf, will lie down together (Isa 11:6). Nations will beat their swords into plowshares and not train for war again (Isa 2:4).

The Hebrew word for peace is *shalom*. It is not just the absence of conflict and war. It is rather a state of total well-being and wholeness, the condition of justice, goodness, joy, and security. The coming of Jesus is interpreted by New Testament writers as the coming of that peace that only God can give. Throughout Paul's writings, God is known as "the God of peace," and the good news of Jesus is called "the gospel of peace" (Eph 6:15). Indeed, Jesus himself is "our peace" (Eph 2:14).

Jesus was able to fall asleep in a ship surrounded by the storm on the sea. In the garden, Jesus urged Peter to put away his sword as Jesus peacefully surrendered his life to his captors. The deep peace of Jesus did not come from an absence of trouble. Jesus had an interior peace that was the result of his trusting relationship with his Father, and he promised to give us that peace when we choose to follow him. Jesus made peace through the blood of his cross (Col 1:20), and through that cross we can have peace with God (Rom 5:1) and with one another. His wounds bring peace to a wounded world.

In his last discourse to his disciples, Jesus urged them not to be afraid or to let their hearts be troubled. He said, "Peace I leave with you; my peace I give to you" (John 14:27). At his resurrection, his first greeting was "Peace be with you" (John 20:19), but then he showed his disciples his hands and his side as a reminder of the great price the Prince of Peace has paid for us. Jesus came to bring peace and he promised to leave us with the means to peace. The Holy Spirit wants to make us more like Jesus, and "the fruit of the Spirit is love, joy, peace" (Gal 5:22). The more we become like Jesus, the more we experience his peace and can share it with others.

Reflection and discussion

• In what areas of my own life do I need the peace of Christ?

• How would I describe peace as it is spoken of in the New Testement?

• How does the life of Jesus demonstrate that peace is not just the absence of trouble?

• What am I really saying when I offer a sign of the peace of Christ to another in the liturgy?

• What do I need to do to cooperate with God's Spirit who brings peace and to receive the gift of peace that only God can give?

• Why is it so difficult, or maybe impossible, for the world to offer peace? What does the world have to learn from Jesus about making peace?

Prayer

Prince of Peace, you came to bring peace on earth, but the world did not receive your message. Help me realize that peace comes from within myself, not from the outside. Help me accept your Spirit of peace and share that peace with others.

Moses said, "The Lord your God will raise up for you from your own people a prophet like me." Acts 3:22

The Prophet

LUKE 4:16–24 ¹⁶ *When he came to Nazareth, where he had been brought up, he went to the synagogue on the sabbath day, as was his custom. He stood up to read,* ¹⁷ *and the scroll of the prophet Isaiah was given to him. He unrolled the scroll and found the place where it was written:*

¹⁸ *"The Spirit of the Lord is upon me,*
because he has anointed me
to bring good news to the poor.
He has sent me to proclaim release to the captives
and recovery of sight to the blind,
to let the oppressed go free,
¹⁹ *to proclaim the year of the Lord's favor."*

²⁰ *And he rolled up the scroll, gave it back to the attendant, and sat down. The eyes of all in the synagogue were fixed on him.* ²¹ *Then he began to say to them, "Today this scripture has been fulfilled in your hearing."* ²² *All spoke well of him and were amazed at the gracious words that came from his mouth. They said, "Is not this Joseph's son?"* ²³ *He said to them, "Doubtless you will quote to me this proverb, 'Doctor, cure yourself!' And you will say 'Do here also in your home town the things that we have heard you did at Capernaum.'"* ²⁴ *And he said, "Truly I tell you, no prophet is accepted in the prophet's hometown."*

ACTS 3:22–26 [22]*Moses said, "The Lord your God will raise up for you from your own people a prophet like me. You must listen to whatever he tells you.* [23]*And it will be that everyone who does not listen to that prophet will be utterly rooted out of the people." * [24]*And all the prophets, as many as have spoken, from Samuel and those after him, also predicted these days.* [25]*You are the descendants of the prophets and of the covenant that God gave to your ancestors, saying to Abraham, 'And in your descendants all the families of the earth shall be blessed.'* [26]*When God raised up his servant, he sent him first to you, to bless you by turning each of you from your wicked ways."*

Jesus is called a prophet in all the gospels. As Jesus raised the widow's son at Nain, the crowd exclaimed, "A great prophet has arisen among us!" (Luke 7:16). The Samaritan woman said to him, "Sir, I see that you are a prophet" (John 4:19). Likewise, the man whose blind eyes had been opened by Jesus said, "He is a prophet" (John 9:17). Jesus entered Jerusalem and the people asked, "Who is this?" The crowds replied, "This is the prophet Jesus from Nazareth in Galilee" (Matt 21:11). And in one of the few sayings preserved in all four gospels, Jesus applies the proverb about the rejected prophet to himself: "No prophet is accepted in the prophet's hometown" (Luke 4:24).

The ministry of Jesus was preceded by that of John the Baptist, clearly a prophet who modeled his life on the prophetic tradition of ancient Israel. John came to prepare the way of the Lord and to preach the message of repentance. When Jesus came to John at the Jordan River, he received a vision that inaugurated his public ministry in much the same way as the inaugural visions received by the Old Testament prophets (Matt 3:13–17). The Spirit that Jesus received at his baptism was understood in the Jewish context as the spirit of God that made one a prophet.

In Deuteronomy, Moses had proclaimed that God promised to raise up for his people "a prophet like you from among their own people." About this future prophet, God said, "I will put my words in the mouth of the prophet, who shall speak to them everything I command" (Deut 18:18). Luke's writings demonstrate that this office of prophet is fulfilled and completed in Jesus. He is the raised prophet foretold through Moses whom Israel was expecting in the last days (Acts 3:22; 7:37).

A prophet, in the Hebrew and Christian tradition, is one who speaks for God, not someone who predicts the future. The prophet is a chosen messenger or representative of God, whose role is to speak God's words and perform miraculous or symbolic acts for the people. The prophetic ministry of Jesus, "a prophet mighty in deed and word" (Luke 24:19), continues through the words and deeds of his apostles. The gift of the Spirit to the Church is manifested through the gift of prophecy, and all those who receive the gift of the Spirit come to share in the gift of prophecy (Acts 2:17–18).

Reflection and discussion

• What are the primary elements of Jesus' mission according to the scroll of Isaiah (Luke 4:18)? What is the source of his mission?

• How does Jesus challenge me with his prophetic message?

• Why does Jesus say, "No prophet is accepted in the prophet's hometown"? Does this explain why it is often necessary for young adults to leave for a while the town in which they were raised?

• Where do I find it most difficult for my unique gifts to be appreciated? How do I deal with feelings of rejection?

• In what ways does the Church continue the mighty words and deeds of its prophetic founder?

• In what ways might I be called to partake in the ministry of the prophet?

Prayer

Jesus, you call me to share in your ministry as prophet. Give me the courage to speak an unpopular message when it is needed and to do what might not be acceptable to those who follow the crowd.

We wait for the blessed hope and the manifestation of the glory of our great God and Savior, Jesus Christ. Titus 2:13

Savior

LUKE 1:68–75 ⁶⁸*"Blessed be the Lord God of Israel,*
for he has looked favourably on his people and redeemed them.
⁶⁹*He has raised up a mighty savior for us*
in the house of his servant David,
⁷⁰*as he spoke through the mouth of his holy prophets from of old,*
⁷¹*that we would be saved from our enemies*
and from the hand of all who hate us.
⁷²*Thus he has shown the mercy promised to our ancestors,*
and has remembered his holy covenant,
⁷³*the oath that he swore to our ancestor Abraham,*
to grant us ⁷⁴*that we, being rescued from the hands of our enemies,*
might serve him without fear, ⁷⁵*in holiness and righteousness*
before him all our days."

TITUS 2:11–14 ¹¹*For the grace of God has appeared, bringing salvation to all,* ¹²*training us to renounce impiety and worldly passions, and in the present age to live lives that are self-controlled, upright, and godly,* ¹³*while we wait for the blessed hope and the manifestation of the glory of our great God and Savior, Jesus Christ.* ¹⁴*He it is who gave himself for us that he might redeem us from all iniquity and purify for himself a people of his own who are zealous for good deeds.*

I n the Old Testament, "salvation" is an event in which people are rescued from a great danger or intolerable situation—one from which they are unable to save themselves. That danger could be political oppression, injustice, military disaster, or physical illness. The God of Israel became known as the saving God based on his mighty act of rescuing the Israelites from slavery in Egypt and bringing them into the Promised Land. God was experienced as Savior again and again throughout history. Though God's salvation was experienced through human instruments, Israel came to realize that no human deliverance could compare with the salvation that God gives (Ps 44:1–8). No other gods or idols could be a savior: "There is no other god besides me, a righteous God and a Savior" (Isa 45:21). Though Israel experienced God as Savior through many historical events, God's promises were never completely fulfilled, and God's people continued to anticipate the fullness of God's salvation in the future.

In the age in which Caesar Augustus was proclaimed as "savior of the world," the angel declared to the shepherds of Bethlehem that "a Savior" was born (Luke 2:11). Zechariah sang that God had raised up "a mighty savior for us" (Luke 1:69) and proclaimed the fulfillment of God's promises that "we would be saved from our enemies and from the hand of all who hate us" (Luke 1:71). This mighty Savior is Jesus, who will bring salvation from the most hated of all enemies: sin and death.

John's gospel announces that God sent Jesus into the world "that the world might be saved through him" (John 3:17). After Jesus preached to the Samaritans, they proclaimed of him, "This is truly the Savior of the world" (John 4:42). In the gospels when Jesus proclaimed: "Your faith has saved you," whether it be from sins, leprosy, demons, or blindness, it means that an enslaving condition has been lifted through the power of Jesus the Savior.

The death and resurrection brings the great biblical story of salvation to its climax. The rejected, crucified Savior is raised and exalted, and proclaimed by the apostles as the "Leader and Savior" who grants repentance and forgiveness (Acts 5:31). The image of Jesus the Savior is so closely joined to God the Savior that, in the letter to Titus, the two are joined as one: "the great God" and "our savior Jesus Christ" (Titus 2:13).

Reflection and discussion

• What is God able to do for me that I cannot do for myself?

• Do I trust Jesus to be my Savior in times of weakness and hopelessness?

• Who are the instruments of God's salvation today? Am I such an instrument of God?

Prayer

Jesus my Savior, you came to bring salvation to all the world. Free me from all that prevents me from being fully alive. I want to receive you as the Savior of my life so that I can experience the forgiveness and freedom you want for me.

SUGGESTIONS FOR FACILITATORS, GROUP SESSION 3

1. Welcome group members and ask if there are any announcements anyone would like to make.

2. You may want to pray this prayer as a group:

Lord Jesus, we gather as your disciples who want to know you more fully. The Scriptures announce that you are Son of Man, Firstborn of God, Emmanuel, Prince of Peace, Prophet, and Savior. You are the giver of all good gifts and the source of those things that we most deeply desire. As we call to you by your many names, work powerfully among us, heal us from all that oppresses us, and help us encourage one another. Send your Holy Spirit upon us and strengthen us with your word.

3. Ask one or more of the following questions:

   • Which names of Jesus so far speak most powerfully to you?

   • What is the most important lesson you learned through your study this week?

4. Discuss lessons 7 through 12. Choose one or more of the questions for reflection and discussion from each lesson to discuss as a group. You may want to ask group members which question was most challenging or helpful to them as you review each lesson.

5. Remember that there are no definitive answers for these discussion questions. The insights of group members will add to the understanding of all. None of these questions requires an expert.

6. After talking about each lesson, instruct group members to complete lessons 13 through 18 on their own during the six days before the next group meeting. They should write out their own answers to the questions as preparation for next week's group discussion.

7. Ask the group if anyone is having any particular problems with the Bible study during the week. You may want to share advice and encouragement within the group.

8. Conclude by praying aloud together the prayer at the end of one of the lessons discussed. You may add to the prayer based on the sharing that has occurred in the group.

"For God so loved the world that he gave his only Son." John 3:16

Son of God

JOHN 3:16–21 [16]*"For God so loved the world that he gave his only Son, so that everyone who believes in him may not perish but may have eternal life.* [17]*"Indeed, God did not send the Son into the world to condemn the world, but in order that the world might be saved through him.* [18]*Those who believe in him are not condemned; but those who do not believe are condemned already, because they have not believed in the name of the only Son of God.* [19]*And this is the judgment, that the light has come into the world, and people loved darkness rather than light because their deeds were evil.* [20]*For all who do evil hate the light and do not come to the light, so that their deeds may not be exposed.* [21]*But those who do what is true come to the light, so that it may be clearly seen that their deeds have been done in God."*

GALATIANS 4:1–7 [1]*My point is this: heirs, as long as they are minors, are no better than slaves, though they are the owners of all the property;* [2]*but they remain under guardians and trustees until the date set by the father.* [3]*So with us; while we were minors, we were enslaved to the elemental spirits of the world.* [4]*But when the fullness of time had come, God sent his Son, born of a woman, born under the law,* [5]*in order to redeem those who were under the law, so that we might receive adoption as children.* [6]*And because you are children, God has sent the Spirit of his Son into our hearts, crying, "Abba! Father!"* [7]*So you are no longer a slave but a child, and if a child then also an heir, through God.*

The designation of Jesus as the Son of God is rooted in the soil of ancient Israel. In Exodus, God named Israel as his son: "Israel is my firstborn son....Let my son go that he may worship me" (Exod 4:22–23). The image is echoed in Hosea: "When Israel was a child I loved him, and out of Egypt I called my son" (Hos 11:1). The kings in the line of David were singled out for a special status as sons of God. God had promised David's descendants, "I will be a father to him, and he shall be a son to me" (2 Sam 7:14). God declared of Israel's king, "You are my son; today I have begotten you" (Ps 2:7).

Jesus came into the world as an Israelite and as a descendant of David. Both of these designations carry the legacy of divine sonship. Yet, while the sonship of Israel and her kings was fraught with disobedience and neglect, Jesus was an obedient and faithful Son living an intimate relationship with his Father. More significantly, Jesus possessed a uniquely intimate sonship with God (John 1:18), which was reflected in his addressing God as "Abba, Father." Of this closeness, Jesus was able to say, "All things have been handed over to me by my Father; and no one knows the Son except the Father, and no one knows the Father except the Son and anyone to whom the Son chooses to reveal him" (Matt 11:27).

The divine person of the Son of God is not a created being who owes his existence to the Father. He has been with God the Father and the Holy Spirit and equal to them from all eternity. The gospel of John calls Jesus God's "only son" (John 1:14, 18; 3:16, 18). He has a unique intimacy with God that is different from that of all others. Yet, as Jesus reveals the Father to us, we are invited to participate in this intimacy with the Father, to come into the family of God. Paul says that we too become God's children: "All who are led by the Spirit of God are children of God" (Rom 8:14). God sent his Son so that we might become adopted children of God, able to call God our Father, becoming true heirs of his promises (Gal 4:4–7).

Reflection and discussion

• What does it mean to me to call God "Abba, Father"? What does it mean to be God's adopted child?

• How do I feel about the invitation to share in God's family life? What are my responsibilities as a son or daughter of God?

• If we are truly brothers and sisters in the same family of God, what does that imply about my relationship to people of other races and nations?

Prayer

Son of God, you show me the way to the house of my Father. Thank you for making me a co-heir with you of all the promises of the Father. Help me see those around me as members of God's family and as my sisters and brothers.

"Here is my servant, whom I have chosen, my beloved, with whom my soul is well pleased." Matt 12:18

God's Servant

ISAIAH 52:13—53:12 ¹³*See, my servant shall prosper;*
he shall be exalted and lifted up,
and shall be very high.
¹⁴*Just as there were many who were astonished at him*
—so marred was his appearance, beyond human semblance,
and his form beyond that of mortals—
¹⁵*so he shall startle many nations;*
kings shall shut their mouths because of him;
for that which had not been told them they shall see,
and that which they had not heard they shall contemplate.

53 ¹*Who has believed what we have heard?*
And to whom has the arm of the Lord been revealed?
²*For he grew up before him like a young plant,*
and like a root out of dry ground;
he had no form or majesty that we should look at him,
nothing in his appearance that we should desire him.
³*He was despised and rejected by others;*
a man of suffering and acquainted with infirmity;

and as one from whom others hide their faces
　　he was despised, and we held him of no account.

[4]Surely he has borne our infirmities
　　and carried our diseases;
yet we accounted him stricken,
　　struck down by God, and afflicted.
[5]But he was wounded for our transgressions,
　　crushed for our iniquities;
upon him was the punishment that made us whole,
　　and by his bruises we are healed.
[6]All we like sheep have gone astray;
　　we have all turned to our own way,
and the Lord has laid on him
　　the iniquity of us all.
[7]He was oppressed, and he was afflicted,
　　yet he did not open his mouth;
like a lamb that is led to the slaughter,
　　and like a sheep that before its shearers is silent,
　　so he did not open his mouth.
[8]By a perversion of justice he was taken away.
　　Who could have imagined his future?
For he was cut off from the land of the living,
　　stricken for the transgression of my people.
[9]They made his grave with the wicked
　　and his tomb with the rich,
although he had done no violence,
　　and there was no deceit in his mouth.

[10]Yet it was the will of the Lord to crush him with pain.
When you make his life an offering for sin,
　　he shall see his offspring, and shall prolong his days;
through him the will of the Lord shall prosper.
　　[11]Out of his anguish he shall see light;
he shall find satisfaction through his knowledge.
　　The righteous one, my servant, shall make many righteous,

and he shall bear their iniquities.
¹²*Therefore I will allot him a portion with the great,*
and he shall divide the spoil with the strong;
because he poured out himself to death,
and was numbered with the transgressors;
yet he bore the sin of many,
and made intercession for the transgressors.

MATTHEW 12:14–21 ¹⁴*But the Pharisees went out and conspired against him, how to destroy him.*

¹⁵*When Jesus became aware of this, he departed. Many crowds followed him, and he cured all of them,* ¹⁶*and he ordered them not to make him known.* ¹⁷*This was to fulfill what had been spoken through the prophet Isaiah:*
¹⁸*"Here is my servant, whom I have chosen,*
my beloved, with whom my soul is well pleased.
I will put my Spirit upon him,
and he will proclaim justice to the Gentiles.
¹⁹*He will not wrangle or cry aloud,*
nor will anyone hear his voice in the streets.
²⁰*He will not break a bruised reed*
or quench a smoldering wick
until he brings justice to victory.
²¹*And in his name the Gentiles will hope."*

J esus is called God's servant in reference to the servant songs of the prophet Isaiah. Four songs in Isaiah 40—55 refer to an anonymous servant who seems to be a person representing both Israel and God (Isa 42:1–4; 49:1–6; 50:4–9; 52:13—53:12). This servant has the qualities of both a prophet and a king. The servant stands quiet and strong, empowered by God's spirit to bring justice to the nations (Isa 42:1–6; Matt 12:18–21).

The final servant song (Isa 52:13–53:12) is most significant in anticipating the suffering ministry of Jesus. The servant suffers for the sins of all, and like the scapegoat of Israel's atonement ritual, his suffering removes the sins of others (Isa 53:4–6, 12). Though the report of his suffering and death shocks and dismays those who hear of it, his vindication hints at resurrection (Isa 52:13; 53:10–11).

The writer of the servant songs may have intended the servant to be a messianic figure. Clearly the person who most fulfills the description of this suffering servant is Jesus. The early Church used these texts to develop its understanding of the atoning suffering and death of Christ. Jesus speaks of his ministry and alludes to his approaching death in these words: "The Son of Man came not to be served but to serve, and to give his life a ransom for many" (Mark 10:45). Jesus is identifying himself with the servant of Isaiah's songs and proclaiming the meaning of his life for the sake of those who will follow him. As disciples of God's suffering servant, we are called to serve others, pouring out our lives in union with Christ, offering ourselves for the good of other people.

Reflection and discussion

• What sufferings of my life can I join to those of Christ on the cross?

• In what specific ways can I be a servant in order to better respond to the needs of others in my family, neighborhood, and community?

Prayer

Suffering Servant of God, you gave your life as a ransom for my own and won for me the fullness of life. Help me to imitate your humble service and join my suffering to yours on the cross.

"I am the good shepherd. The good shepherd lays down his life for the sheep." John 10:11

Good Shepherd

JOHN 10:1–18 [1]*"Very truly, I tell you, anyone who does not enter the sheep-fold by the gate but climbs in by another way is a thief and a bandit.* [2]*The one who enters by the gate is the shepherd of the sheep.* [3]*The gatekeeper opens the gate for him, and the sheep hear his voice. He calls his own sheep by name and leads them out.* [4]*When he has brought out all his own, he goes ahead of them, and the sheep follow him because they know his voice.* [5]*They will not follow a stranger, but they will run from him because they do not know the voice of strangers."* [6]*Jesus used this figure of speech with them, but they did not understand what he was saying to them.*

[7]*So again Jesus said to them, "Very truly, I tell you, I am the gate for the sheep.* [8]*All who came before me are thieves and bandits; but the sheep did not listen to them.* [9]*I am the gate. Whoever enters by me will be saved, and will come in and go out and find pasture.* [10]*The thief comes only to steal and kill and destroy. I came that they may have life, and have it abundantly.*

[11]*"I am the good shepherd. The good shepherd lays down his life for the sheep.* [12]*The hired hand, who is not the shepherd and does not own the sheep, sees the wolf coming and leaves the sheep and runs away—and the wolf snatches them and scatters them.* [13]*The hired hand runs away because a hired hand does not care for the sheep.* [14]*I am the good shepherd. I know my own and my own know*

me, [15]just as the Father knows me and I know the Father. And I lay down my life for the sheep. [16]I have other sheep that do not belong to this fold. I must bring them also, and they will listen to my voice. So there will be one flock, one shepherd. [17]For this reason the Father loves me, because I lay down my life in order to take it up again. [18]No one takes it from me, but I lay it down of my own accord. I have power to lay it down, and I have power to take it up again. I have received this command from my Father."

1 PETER 5:1–4 *[1]Now as an elder myself and a witness of the sufferings of Christ, as well as one who shares in the glory to be revealed, I exhort the elders among you [2]to tend the flock of God that is in your charge, exercising the oversight, not under compulsion but willingly, as God would have you do it—not for sordid gain but eagerly. [3]Do not lord it over those in your charge, but be examples to the flock. [4]And when the chief shepherd appears, you will win the crown of glory that never fades away.*

Jesus' identification of himself as the good shepherd in John's gospel is rooted in the Old Testament. Shepherds, as described throughout the Bible, provided their flocks with food and water, defended them against wild animals and thieves, stayed with them night and day, and searched for those who wandered astray. Kings, priests, and prophets of Israel are described as faithful or wicked shepherds.

God is frequently spoken of in the Old Testament as the shepherd who guides his people (Ps 23:1–4; Isa 40:11). Ezekiel 34:11–16 presents God as the future shepherd, gathering his flock after the exile: "I will seek the lost, and I will bring back the strayed, and I will bind up the injured, and I will strengthen the weak" (Ezek 34:16). The prophets also spoke of a future Davidic Messiah who would shepherd God's people; there would be "one shepherd" who would form "one flock" (Ezek 34:23; Micah 5:4).

Jesus is the good shepherd who calls each sheep by its own familiar name. When they hear the shepherd's voice, they follow him and he walks ahead of them to lead them (John 10:3–4). Jesus is the messianic shepherd of the Old Testament prophets, yet he expands their expectation by proclaiming: "The good shepherd lays down his life for the sheep" (verse 11). Jesus further astounds his Jewish audience by stating that he will gather other sheep who are outside the fold. They too will hear his voice and he will lead them so that "there will be one flock, one shepherd" (verse 16) for all the people of God.

Peter's first letter exhorts all the leaders of God's Church to imitate Jesus the good shepherd in their care of God's people (1 Pet 5:1–4). The Church has had lots of painful experiences with false shepherds. One who does not pastor in imitation of Jesus is nothing more than "a thief and a bandit" or a "hired hand" (John 10:1, 12–13). False shepherds are minimally invested in the flock and do not protect the sheep from harm. The true pastor, on the other hand, is trusted by the sheep because he speaks God's word and risks his own life for their welfare.

Reflection and discussion

• What are the characteristics of faithful shepherds as described in the Bible?

• What characteristics of Jesus, the Good Shepherd, were most surprising to his listeners?

• How have I experienced Jesus acting in my life as a good shepherd?

• Name three characteristics of pastoral leadership mentioned in Peter's first letter.

• What are the characteristics of a false shepherd? Why are these characteristics so scandalous?

• In what situation have I been called to be a shepherd-leader? What can I learn about shepherding and leadership from these passages?

Prayer

Good Shepherd of God's flock, you guide my life and provide all that I need. As you call me by name, help me listen to your voice and trust that you will protect me and lead me to abundant pastures.

"As long as I am in the world, I am the light of the world." John 9:5

Light of the World

JOHN 9:1–7 ¹*As he walked along, he saw a man blind from birth. ²His disciples asked him, "Rabbi, who sinned, this man or his parents, that he was born blind?" ³Jesus answered, "Neither this man nor his parents sinned; he was born blind so that God's works might be revealed in him. ⁴We must work the works of him who sent me while it is day; night is coming when no one can work. ⁵As long as I am in the world, I am the light of the world." ⁶When he had said this, he spat on the ground and made mud with the saliva and spread the mud on the man's eyes, ⁷saying to him, "Go, wash in the pool of Siloam" (which means Sent). Then he went and washed and came back able to see.*

EPHESIANS 5:6–14 ⁶*Let no one deceive you with empty words, for because of these things the wrath of God comes on those who are disobedient. ⁷Therefore do not be associated with them. ⁸For once you were darkness, but now in the Lord you are light. Live as children of light— ⁹for the fruit of the light is found in all that is good and right and true. ¹⁰Try to find out what is pleasing to the Lord. ¹¹Take no part in the unfruitful works of darkness, but instead expose them. ¹²For it is shameful even to mention what such people do secretly; ¹³but everything exposed by the light becomes visible, ¹⁴for everything that becomes visible is light.*

Therefore it says,
  "Sleeper, awake!
    Rise from the dead,
  and Christ will shine on you."

The prologue of John's gospel describes Jesus as "the light of all people," the light that "shines in the darkness" (John 1:4–5), the "true light which enlightens everyone" (John 1:9). In an age in which light is accessible at the flip of a switch, it is easy to overlook the fact that in the ancient world, light was something imbued with mystery. In the Old Testament, light often represents a manifestation of God or the good things that came from God: prosperity, blessings, and salvation. "The Lord is my light," said Micah (7:8); God is "the Light of Israel," proclaimed Isaiah (10:17). The prophets associated the light of God's presence especially with the new age to come: "The Lord will be your everlasting light" (Isa 60:19–20).

Matthew tells us that Jesus began his ministry in order to fulfill what had been spoken by Isaiah: "The people who sat in darkness have seen a great light, and for those who sat in the region and shadow of death, light has dawned" (Matt 4:16). John's gospel situates Jesus' manifestation as "light of the world" within the context of the Jewish feast of Tabernacles. Huge torches were lit in the temple courtyard symbolizing that the Torah of Israel and the temple of Jerusalem were light for God's people. At the feast, Jesus fulfilled and universalized the Jewish symbolism, proclaiming: "I am the light of the world. Whoever follows me will never walk in darkness but will have the light of life" (John 8:12). Leaving the Temple, Jesus sees a man who had been blind since his birth. The light of the world gave sight and faith to the man who had never seen the light (John 9:1–7).

The light of Christ shines upon us and within us, showing us the truth about ourselves. That light of truth shines into every part of us, enabling us to see the things that need to be changed and also showing us the things God wants to affirm. As believers in Jesus, we are called to let the light of Christ shine from within us to all the world (Matt 5:14–16), to be "light in the Lord," to be "children of light" (Eph 5:8). Like individual tapers lit from the Easter candle, we fill the world with the light that scatters the darkness.

Reflection and discussion

• What parts of my life are still in the darkness?

• What parts of myself shine more brightly when reflecting the light of Christ?

• What do I need Christ to open my eyes to so that I may live as a child of light?

Prayer

Light of the world, you shine your light into the darkness and open the eyes of the blind. Show me the light that I have never known since my birth so that your light may shine brightly through me.

"Here is the Lamb of God who takes away the sin of the world!"
John 1:29

Lamb of God

JOHN 1:29–37 [29]*The next day John the Baptist saw Jesus coming towards him and declared, "Here is the Lamb of God who takes away the sin of the world!* [30]*This is he of whom I said, 'After me comes a man who ranks ahead of me because he was before me.'* [31]*I myself did not know him; but I came baptizing with water for this reason, that he might be revealed to Israel."* [32]*And John testified, "I saw the Spirit descending from heaven like a dove, and it remained on him.* [33]*I myself did not know him, but the one who sent me to baptize with water said to me, 'He on whom you see the Spirit descend and remain is the one who baptizes with the Holy Spirit.'* [34]*And I myself have seen and have testified that this is the Son of God."*

[35]*The next day John again was standing with two of his disciples,* [36]*and as he watched Jesus walk by, he exclaimed, "Look, here is the Lamb of God!"* [37]*The two disciples heard him say this, and they followed Jesus.*

REVELATION 5:6–14 [6]*Then I saw between the throne and the four living creatures and among the elders a Lamb standing as if it had been slaughtered, having seven horns and seven eyes, which are the seven spirits of God sent out into all the earth.* [7]*He went and took the scroll from the right hand of the one who was* *seated on the throne. ⁸When he had taken the scroll, the four living creatures and the twenty-four elders fell before the Lamb, each holding a harp and golden bowls full of incense, which are the prayers of the saints. ⁹They sing a new song: "You are worthy to take the scroll and to open its seals, for you were slaughtered and by your blood you ransomed for God saints from every tribe and language and people and nation; ¹⁰you have made them to be a kingdom and priests serving our God, and they will reign on earth." ¹¹Then I looked, and I heard the voice of many angels surrounding the throne and the living creatures and the elders; they numbered myriads of myriads and thousands of thousands, ¹²singing with full voice, "Worthy is the Lamb that was slaughtered to receive power and wealth and wisdom and might and honor and glory and blessing!" ¹³Then I heard every creature in heaven and on earth and under the earth and in the sea, and all that is in them, singing, "To the one seated on the throne and to the Lamb be blessing and honor and glory and might forever and ever!" ¹⁴And the four living creatures said, "Amen!" And the elders fell down and worshipped.*

Jesus' designation by John the Baptist as the Lamb of God who takes away the world's sin is rooted in the ritual practice of ancient Israel. Lambs are mentioned in connection with sacrifices more than eighty times in Exodus, Leviticus, and Numbers. At the Passover, the blood of a lamb saved each household of Israel; lambs were offered in sacrifice each morning and evening and at major feasts; and the suffering servant gave his life as an offering for sin "like a lamb led to the slaughter" (Isa 53:7, 10).

The title, Lamb of God, describes Jesus as the one through whom God will take away sin. The ancient means for gaining forgiveness and union with God has been transcended. Jesus is the Passover lamb, the sin offering, the communion sacrifice, the final victim. The sacrifices of old were fulfilled and perfected when Christ died for the sins of the world.

Jesus is God's Lamb, the Lamb sent by God as the perfect sacrifice. At Passover, the Israelites were told by God to choose a lamb that was without blemish (Exod 12:5), an offering as perfect as possible. In the death of Jesus on the cross, the whole people of God gain redemption through "the precious blood of Christ, like that of a lamb without defect or blemish" (1 Pet 1:19).

In the book of Revelation, the Lamb is the dominant image for Jesus. The triumphal Lamb holds the fullness of power (seven horns) and perfect wisdom (seven eyes), yet still bears the marks of its slaughter (Rev 5:6). He is risen and his glorious wounds are evident for all to see. The Lamb of God pointed out by John is now worshipped by all of heaven and earth: "Worthy is the Lamb that was slaughtered" (Rev 5:12). He alone is worthy to open the scroll with its seven seals. Only the glorified Lamb could open the book of God's eternal decrees for human history and put them into effect. He is the one who brings God's plan for the world to its completion and thus is worshiped eternally by all creation.

Reflection and discussion

• Why is the title "Lamb of God" such an ideal image to describe the redeeming work of Jesus?

• What are the implications for my life if the sacrifice of Jesus truly atoned for all my sins?

• In what ways have the wounds of my life been transformed and glorified?

Prayer

Eternal Lamb of God, you are indeed worthy to receive honor, glory, and might. With your blood you purchased me for God and redeemed my life. I will praise you always with all the angels and saints of heaven.

"I am the bread of life. Whoever comes to me will never be hungry."
John 6:35

Bread of Life

JOHN 6:30–59 ³⁰*So they said to Jesus, "What sign are you going to give us then, so that we may see it and believe you? What work are you performing?* ³¹*Our ancestors ate the manna in the wilderness; as it is written, 'He gave them bread from heaven to eat.'"* ³²*Then Jesus said to them, "Very truly, I tell you, it was not Moses who gave you the bread from heaven, but it is my Father who gives you the true bread from heaven.* ³³*For the bread of God is that which comes down from heaven and gives life to the world."* ³⁴*They said to him, "Sir, give us this bread always."*

³⁵*Jesus said to them, "I am the bread of life. Whoever comes to me will never be hungry, and whoever believes in me will never be thirsty.* ³⁶*But I said to you that you have seen me and yet do not believe.* ³⁷*Everything that the Father gives me will come to me, and anyone who comes to me I will never drive away;* ³⁸*for I have come down from heaven, not to do my own will, but the will of him who sent me.* ³⁹*And this is the will of him who sent me, that I should lose nothing of all that he has given me, but raise it up on the last day.* ⁴⁰*This is indeed the will of my Father, that all who see the Son and believe in him may have eternal life; and I will raise them up on the last day."*

⁴¹*Then the Jews began to complain about him because he said, "I am the bread that came down from heaven."* ⁴²*They were saying, "Is not this Jesus, the son of*

Joseph, whose father and mother we know? How can he now say, 'I have come down from heaven'?" ⁴³Jesus answered them, "Do not complain among yourselves. ⁴⁴No one can come to me unless drawn by the Father who sent me; and I will raise that person up on the last day. ⁴⁵It is written in the prophets, 'And they shall all be taught by God.' Everyone who has heard and learned from the Father comes to me. ⁴⁶Not that anyone has seen the Father except the one who is from God; he has seen the Father. ⁴⁷Very truly, I tell you, whoever believes has eternal life. ⁴⁸I am the bread of life. ⁴⁹Your ancestors ate the manna in the wilderness, and they died. ⁵⁰This is the bread that comes down from heaven, so that one may eat of it and not die. ⁵¹I am the living bread that came down from heaven. Whoever eats of this bread will live forever; and the bread that I will give for the life of the world is my flesh."

⁵²The Jews then disputed among themselves, saying, "How can this man give us his flesh to eat?" ⁵³So Jesus said to them, "Very truly, I tell you, unless you eat the flesh of the Son of Man and drink his blood, you have no life in you. ⁵⁴Those who eat my flesh and drink my blood have eternal life, and I will raise them up on the last day; ⁵⁵for my flesh is true food and my blood is true drink. ⁵⁶Those who eat my flesh and drink my blood abide in me, and I in them. ⁵⁷Just as the living Father sent me, and I live because of the Father, so whoever eats me will live because of me. ⁵⁸This is the bread that came down from heaven, not like that which your ancestors ate, and they died. But the one who eats this bread will live forever." ⁵⁹He said these things while he was teaching in the synagogue at Capernaum.

In the gospel of John, after Jesus feeds the hungry crowds with bread and fish, he proclaims, "I am the bread of life," bringing together all the major biblical themes associated with bread. Bread was the most basic component of first-century meals; often bread was synonymous with food. Just as it would be impossible to sustain life without bread, so too, Jesus implies, it is impossible to live an abundant life apart from the spiritual sustenance he provides as the bread of life.

Bread is even more importantly a gift of God. As early as patriarchal times, bread became a symbol of hospitality, to be shared by strangers and friends alike, as we see in the account of Melchizedek (Gen 14:18). A table with twelve loaves of bread, the bread of the presence, was daily displayed before the Holy of Holies (Exod 25:30). That God is the giver of bread is expressed most dramatically when the Israelites hungered in the desert. God provided manna each day, "the bread that the Lord has given you to eat" (Exod 16:15). Jesus says that in contrast to God's gift given through Moses, "It is my Father who gives you the true bread from heaven" (John 6:32). The bread of God, Jesus himself, "comes down from heaven and gives life to the world" (John 6:33).

At the Last Supper, Jesus gave thanks for the bread and said, "This is my body, which is given for you" (Luke 22:19). In his sacrificial gift of himself for the world, Jesus becomes the bread of life in the fullness of his person. The discourse in John also associates Jesus as the true bread with the Eucharist: "The bread that I will give for the life of the world is my flesh" (John 6:51, 53). What physical bread is for the body, the bread of life is for our hungry hearts. We are fed with his living word and with his Eucharistic presence. Without him, we suffer malnutrition and starve. He alone can satisfy the truest hungers of humanity and the deepest longings of our lives.

Reflection and discussion

• What is the "daily bread" for which I pray in the "Our Father"?

• What is the content of my daily spiritual diet?

• How can I share bread with those who hunger?

• What promises of Jesus for the those who come to him is repeated three times (verses 40, 44, 54)? What does this mean to me?

• What new insights does the bread of life discourse (John 6) offer me about the Eucharist?

Prayer

Bread of Life, I hunger for the food that can fill my deepest longing and truly satisfy me. Thank you for becoming flesh so that you could give your flesh to us as the bread of eternal life.

SUGGESTIONS FOR FACILITATORS, GROUP SESSION 4

1. Welcome group members and ask if anyone has any questions, announcements, or requests.

2. You may want to pray this prayer as a group:

Jesus, you have given us the teachings of the gospels and called each of us to an intimate life with you. You call us by name, and we call you by your many names. Let us know you more deeply as Son of God, Suffering Servant, Good Shepherd, Light of the World, Lamb of God, and Bread of Life. We come to you with many needs and fears; you promise to shine in our darkness, feed our hungers, forgive our sins, protect us from harm, and lead us to your Father's home. For every name that you wear is a blessing that you share. Lead us with your Spirit to know you more fully.

3. Ask one or more of the following questions:

- What is the most difficult part of this study for you?

- What did you learn about yourself this week?

4. Discuss lessons 13 through 18. Choose one or more of the questions for reflection and discussion from each lesson to discuss as a group. You may want to ask group members which question was most challenging or helpful to them as you review each lesson.

5. Keep the discussion moving, but allow time for the questions that provoke the most discussion. Encourage the group members to use "I" language in their responses.

6. After talking over each lesson, instruct group members to complete lessons 19 through 24 on their own during the six days before the next group meeting. They should write out their own answers to the questions as preparation for next week's session.

7. Ask the group what encouragement they need for the coming week. Ask the members to pray for the needs of one another during the week.

8. Conclude by praying aloud together the prayer at the end of one of the lessons discussed. You may choose to conclude the prayer by asking members to pray aloud any requests they may have.

"I am the resurrection and the life. Those who believe in me, even though they die, will live." John 11:25

The Resurrection and the Life

JOHN 11:17–44 *17 When Jesus arrived, he found that Lazarus had already been in the tomb four days. 18 Now Bethany was near Jerusalem, some two miles away, 19 and many of the Jews had come to Martha and Mary to console them about their brother. 20 When Martha heard that Jesus was coming, she went and met him, while Mary stayed at home. 21 Martha said to Jesus, "Lord, if you had been here, my brother would not have died. 22 But even now I know that God will give you whatever you ask of him." 23 Jesus said to her, "Your brother will rise again." 24 Martha said to him, "I know that he will rise again in the resurrection on the last day." 25 Jesus said to her, "I am the resurrection and the life. Those who believe in me, even though they die, will live, 26 and everyone who lives and believes in me will never die. Do you believe this?" 27 She said to him, "Yes, Lord, I believe that you are the Messiah, the Son of God, the one coming into the world."*

28 When she had said this, she went back and called her sister Mary, and told her privately, "The Teacher is here and is calling for you." 29 And when she heard it, she got up quickly and went to him. 30 Now Jesus had not yet come to the village, but was still at the place where Martha had met him. 31 The Jews who were with her in the house, consoling her, saw Mary get up quickly and go out. They followed her because they thought that she was going to the tomb to weep there. ³²*When Mary came where Jesus was and saw him, she knelt at his feet and said to him, "Lord, if you had been here, my brother would not have died."* ³³*When Jesus saw her weeping, and the Jews who came with her also weeping, he was greatly disturbed in spirit and deeply moved.* ³⁴*He said, "Where have you laid him?" They said to him, "Lord, come and see."* ³⁵*Jesus began to weep.* ³⁶*So the Jews said, "See how he loved him!"* ³⁷*But some of them said, "Could not he who opened the eyes of the blind man have kept this man from dying?"*

³⁸*Then Jesus, again greatly disturbed, came to the tomb. It was a cave, and a stone was lying against it.* ³⁹*Jesus said, "Take away the stone." Martha, the sister of the dead man, said to him, "Lord, already there is a stench because he has been dead four days."* ⁴⁰*Jesus said to her, "Did I not tell you that if you believed, you would see the glory of God?"* ⁴¹*So they took away the stone. And Jesus looked upward and said, "Father, I thank you for having heard me.* ⁴²*I knew that you always hear me, but I have said this for the sake of the crowd standing here, so that they may believe that you sent me."* ⁴³*When he had said this, he cried with a loud voice, "Lazarus, come out!"* ⁴⁴*The dead man came out, his hands and feet bound with strips of cloth, and his face wrapped in a cloth. Jesus said to them, "Unbind him, and let him go."*

The responses of Jesus to Martha and to Mary were quite different. To Martha, Jesus offered an explanation of faith. He brought her from a vague understanding that Lazarus would rise again someday to a belief that Jesus is truly the source of resurrection and life (verses 23–26). Because Jesus is the resurrection, the one who believes in Jesus will live, even though he dies; and because Jesus is the life, the one who lives and believes in Jesus will never ultimately die. Resurrection and eternal life are the fruits of a relationship with Jesus; wherever Jesus is, there is life that never ends.

In response to Mary, who fell at his feet, Jesus expressed deep emotional involvement (verses 33, 35). The emotional reaction of Jesus was one of deep sadness and profound grief for what death has done to his friends, Lazarus, Martha, and Mary. The believing response that Jesus offered Martha and the emotional response he offered Mary represent two necessary and complementary aspects of faith: the response of the mind and the response of the heart.

The way Lazarus emerged from the tomb, "his head and feet bound with strips of cloth and his face wrapped in a cloth" (verse 44), reminds us that the raising of Lazarus is far different from the resurrection of Jesus. The one who is the resurrection and the life will leave the funeral wrappings in the tomb and emerge in total freedom (John 20:6–7). The command of Jesus, "Unbind him and let him go," echoes the command spoken by Moses in the name of God: "Let my people go" (Exod 5:1). God wants his people to be free from all bondage, even the final prison of death, so that we can experience the fullness of God's eternal life. Like the exodus, the raising of Lazarus was a preview of the resurrection in Christ.

Like most of the gospel of John, the account of Lazarus must be read on at least two levels. It is about a man named Lazarus, a dear friend whom Jesus loved. But it is also about each of us, whom Jesus loves, and about the universal fate of death with which we must all sooner or later cope. Lazarus represents all of us as we come to Jesus as the source of life and hope.

Reflection and discussion

• How do I answer the question of Jesus: "Do you believe this?" (verse 26)?

• What emotions do I experience when contemplating the reality of death?

• How do thoughts of my own death lead me to deeper belief?

• What are the different responses Jesus offered to Martha and Mary? Why are both responses necessary?

• In what ways are the raising of Lazarus and the resurrection of Jesus different? How is the raised Lazarus a preview of the risen Jesus?

Prayer

Jesus, you loved your friend Lazarus. Help me experience your tender love for me and comfort me with your assurance as I consider my own inevitable death. Help me believe that you are the resurrection and the life, my ultimate hope and destiny.

"I am the true vine, and my Father is the vine-grower." John 15:1

The True Vine

JOHN 15:1–8 [1] *"I am the true vine, and my Father is the vine-grower. [2] He removes every branch in me that bears no fruit. Every branch that bears fruit he prunes to make it bear more fruit. [3] You have already been cleansed by the word that I have spoken to you. [4] Abide in me as I abide in you. Just as the branch cannot bear fruit by itself unless it abides in the vine, neither can you unless you abide in me. [5] I am the vine, you are the branches. Those who abide in me and I in them bear much fruit, because apart from me you can do nothing. [6] Whoever does not abide in me is thrown away like a branch and withers; such branches are gathered, thrown into the fire, and burned. [7] If you abide in me, and my words abide in you, ask for whatever you wish, and it will be done for you. [8] My Father is glorified by this, that you bear much fruit and become my disciples."*

The self-revelation of Jesus as "the true vine" points to the intimate relationship between Jesus and his Father as well as the intimacy that Jesus shares with his disciples. The fruitful grapevines that grow all over Israel are a frequent image in the Hebrew Scriptures. Isaiah spoke of the vineyard as an image of God's people. Though carefully planted and cultivated by God, the vineyard yielded wild grapes (Isa 5:1–2). Psalm 80 is a song about the vine God brought out of Egypt and planted in the land (Ps 80:8–15).

Jesus uses the grapevine to teach his disciples about the mystical relationship he desires between himself and believers. Notice that Jesus does not say he is the trunk; he is rather the whole vine. We are the branches that make up the vine. We receive life from him not by being merely connected to him; we share in his life by becoming part of him. Jesus not only gives us life, he lives his life in us so that we are fully united with him and live in him. When we are united with Jesus in faith, we actually live with his life and love with his love.

The source of this life and love is the Father, the vine-grower. He "planted" Jesus in our world for the purpose of enabling us to attach to his life and to produce the fruits of love, and he "tends" the vine by guiding Jesus toward his final loving sacrifice. The wise vine-grower knows that the fruitfulness of the vine requires careful pruning. The fruit-bearing branches must be cut away to produce more fruit (verse 2). Vines allowed to grow without pruning will produce smaller and smaller grapes as the vines gradually return to their wild state. The pruning represents the trials and suffering required of those who unite their lives with the loving and total sacrifice of Jesus.

The fruit of the vine is the grape, which, when crushed and fermented, becomes wine. At the Christian Eucharist, the fruit of the vine is the blood of Christ that is poured out for his disciples (Mark 14:23–25). To bear fruit means to do something; it is to show forth the love that is the hallmark of discipleship (John 13:34–35). This fruit of the vine is acts of love done in imitation of and in union with Jesus, who gave his life out of love for us.

This mystical union between Jesus and believers is expressed by the word translated as "abide": "Abide in me as I abide in you" (verse 4). It suggests a deeply personal and lasting union of lives. The branches abide in the vine so that they can bear fruit; the believer abides in Jesus to produce the lasting fruit of unselfish love.

Reflection and discussion

• How does the image of the vine express the mystical relationship between Jesus and us?

• What characteristics does my life have in common with a grapevine? With winemaking?

• Why is pruning so necessary for a vine's fruitfulness? In what ways do I experience pruning in order to grow and bear more fruit?

• What fruit am I bearing because my life is united with Jesus?

Prayer

Fruitful Vine, thank you for uniting your life to mine and for the love you showed in giving your life in sacrifice. Help me accept the necessary pruning and help me bear the fruit of loving service for your people

The stone that the builders rejected has become the chief cornerstone.

Psalm 118:22

The Cornerstone

MARK 12:1–12 ¹*Then Jesus began to speak to them in parables. "A man planted a vineyard, put a fence around it, dug a pit for the wine press, and built a watchtower; then he leased it to tenants and went to another country. ²When the season came, he sent a slave to the tenants to collect from them his share of the produce of the vineyard. ³But they seized him, and beat him, and sent him away empty-handed. ⁴And again he sent another slave to them; this one they beat over the head and insulted. ⁵Then he sent another, and that one they killed. And so it was with many others; some they beat, and others they killed. ⁶He had still one other, a beloved son. Finally he sent him to them, saying, 'They will respect my son.' ⁷But those tenants said to one another, 'This is the heir; come, let us kill him, and the inheritance will be ours.' ⁸So they seized him, killed him, and threw him out of the vineyard. ⁹What then will the owner of the vineyard do? He will come and destroy the tenants and give the vineyard to others. ¹⁰Have you not read this scripture:*

'The stone that the builders rejected
has become the cornerstone;
¹¹this was the Lord's doing,
and it is amazing in our eyes'?"

¹²*When they realized that he had told this parable against them, they wanted to arrest him, but they feared the crowd. So they left him and went away.*

1 PETER 2:4–10 ⁴*Come to him, a living stone, though rejected by mortals yet chosen and precious in God's sight, and* ⁵*like living stones, let yourselves be built into a spiritual house, to be a holy priesthood, to offer spiritual sacrifices acceptable to God through Jesus Christ.* ⁶*For it stands in scripture:*

> *"See, I am laying in Zion a stone,*
>> *a cornerstone chosen and precious;*
> *and whoever believes in him will not be put to shame."*

⁷*To you then who believe, he is precious; but for those who do not believe,*

> *"The stone that the builders rejected*
>> *has become the very head of the corner,"*

⁸*and*

> *"A stone that makes them stumble,*
>> *and a rock that makes them fall."*

They stumble because they disobey the word, as they were destined to do. ⁹*But you are a chosen race, a royal priesthood, a holy nation, God's own people, in order that you may proclaim the mighty acts of him who called you out of darkness into his marvelous light.* ¹⁰*Once you were not a people,*

> *but now you are God's people;*
> *once you had not received mercy,*
> *but now you have received mercy.*

The cornerstone is that stone on which a building most depends for its structural integrity. It may be the cornerstone which is laid first so as to ensure a straight and level foundation; it may be the capstone at the top corner of a wall signaling a building's completion; or it may be the keystone of an arched door or gateway, the topmost stone which joins the two sides and supports the arch.

The cornerstone is used frequently in the Scriptures in a metaphorical sense. As the divine voice from the whirlwind describes the world's creation as the work of a great builder in the book of Job, God asks, "Who laid its cornerstone?" (Job 38:6).

The most frequent use of the image of the cornerstone originates with Psalm 118:22, "The stone that the builders rejected has become the chief cornerstone." The rejected stone originally referred to Israel, rejected by the great nations but chosen by God. Later Judaism interpreted the passage to refer to King David, who was considered most unlikely among Jesse's sons to be king, but chosen by God to be exalted.

This reference to King David explains why Jesus used the passage to elaborate on the parable of the tenants of God's vineyard. The tenants, the ruling priests of the temple, rejected the vineyard owner's son, Jesus (Mark 12:6–8); likewise the stone, Jesus, rejected by the builders, the temple priests, would become the cornerstone (Mark 12:10). Jesus, through his passion and death, would become the foundation of God's restored people, the new and living temple of God.

All who come to Jesus are "living stones" (1 Pet 2:4–5) being built into a new, spiritual edifice for offering sacrifice to God. For the unbelievers, Christ is an obstacle, a stumbling stone on which they will fall (1 Pet 2:8); for the believers, he is the chosen, precious, cornerstone (1 Pet 2:6). The letter to the Ephesians describes the Church as a spiritual temple, with the apostles and prophets as the foundation, being built as a dwelling place for God. Christ is the cornerstone; "in him the whole structure is joined together and grows into a holy temple" (Eph 2:20–22).

As God's holy temple, we depend on Jesus for our structural integrity. The lateral lines of the temple stretch out from the cornerstone, stone by stone, to form the solid walls. The vertical lines reach up toward the sky. Structurally sound, we give glory to God and form that holy edifice from which sacrifice rises to the heavens.

Reflection and discussion

• What are the three possible meanings for the term "cornerstone"? What does each of these have in common?

• How does the rejected stone that became the cornerstone refer to Israel, David, and Jesus?

• Do I stumble and fall over Christ or do I build my life on him?

• Do I fit snugly as a stone in God's spiritual temple or do I need straightening, cutting, or mortar to hold me in place?

Prayer

Christ, you are the cornerstone of God's creation and the precious stone that holds your Church together. Help me join my life to that of your people so that we may offer our prayers, works, joys, and sufferings in union with your perfect sacrifice.

"This is Jesus, the King of the Jews." Matt 27:37

King of the Jews

MATTHEW 27:27–37 ²⁷ *Then the soldiers of the governor took Jesus into the governor's headquarters, and they gathered the whole cohort around him.* ²⁸ *They stripped him and put a scarlet robe on him,* ²⁹ *and after twisting some thorns into a crown, they put it on his head. They put a reed in his right hand and knelt before him and mocked him, saying, "Hail, King of the Jews!"* ³⁰ *They spat on him, and took the reed and struck him on the head.* ³¹ *After mocking him, they stripped him of the robe and put his own clothes on him. Then they led him away to crucify him.*

³² *As they went out, they came upon a man from Cyrene named Simon; they compelled this man to carry his cross.* ³³ *And when they came to a place called Golgotha (which means Place of a Skull),* ³⁴ *they offered him wine to drink, mixed with gall; but when he tasted it, he would not drink it.* ³⁵ *And when they had crucified him, they divided his clothes among themselves by casting lots;* ³⁶ *then they sat down there and kept watch over him.* ³⁷ *Over his head they put the charge against him, which read, "This is Jesus, the King of the Jews."*

JOHN 18:33–40 ³³ *Then Pilate entered the headquarters again, summoned Jesus, and asked him, "Are you the King of the Jews?"* ³⁴ *Jesus answered, "Do you ask this on your own, or did others tell you about me?"* ³⁵ *Pilate replied, "I am not a Jew, am I? Your own nation and the chief priests have handed you over to me.*

What have you done?" [36] *Jesus answered, "My kingdom is not from this world. If my kingdom were from this world, my followers would be fighting to keep me from being handed over to the Jews. But as it is, my kingdom is not from here."* [37] *Pilate asked him, "So you are a king?" Jesus answered, "You say that I am a king. For this I was born, and for this I came into the world, to testify to the truth. Everyone who belongs to the truth listens to my voice."* [38] *Pilate asked him, "What is truth?"*

After he had said this, he went out to the Jews again and told them, "I find no case against him. [39] *But you have a custom that I release someone for you at the Passover. Do you want me to release for you the King of the Jews?"* [40] *They shouted in reply, "Not this man, but Barabbas!" Now Barabbas was a bandit.*

In the account of the trial and crucifixion of Jesus in all four gospels, Jesus is proclaimed as "King of the Jews." At his trial, Pilate asked Jesus, "Are you the kings of the Jews?" (Matt 27:11; John 18:33). In the first three gospels, Jesus answers ambiguously, "You say so." In John's gospel, Jesus responds by speaking about the nature of his kingdom, which is not of this world. He exercises his royalty in witnessing to the truth and draws all those who are of the truth into his kingdom (John 18:36–37). Yet neither the Roman political authority nor the Jewish religious authority is able to recognize the truth that stands before them.

The readers of the gospel know that Jesus is king of heaven and earth, yet not in a worldly sense: "My kingdom is not from here" (John 18:36). Yet, Jesus, bound as a prisoner, possesses a power that easily surpasses the power of Rome and its empire. This new kind of power is expressed in self-effacement, suffering, and generous love. Because the authorities cannot recognize royal power in the pathetic figure of Jesus, they seek to destroy what they cannot understand. Pilate proclaims his own power, the power to release Jesus or to crucify Jesus (John 19:10). Those who rely on the political or religious power of strength and intimidation believe to the end that such power solves problems. They weigh human life on the scales of convenience. Jesus shows that genuine power comes from God and is to be used to serve people: "You would have no power over me unless it had been given you from above" (John 19:11).

The kingship of Jesus is displayed here with dramatic irony: the crown of thorns, the royal robe, and the mocking acclamations. In John's gospel Pilate solemnly displays Jesus to his people with the words, "Here is the man!" (John 19:5). Pilate is presenting Jesus as a pitiful and broken man who should not be taken seriously. Yet, vulnerable and suffering, the true kingship of Jesus was never more clearly displayed. Through this starkly memorable scene, it becomes clear that the most powerful people in the world are not the power brokers of politics and industry, but the humble, often obscure people who are true disciples of Jesus and who make his presence known in the world.

All the gospels note that on the cross was attached the ironic inscription: "Jesus of Nazareth, the King of the Jews" (Matt 27:37; John 19:19). John's gospel describes the notice as a universal, heraldic proclamation, written in Hebrew, the language of religion, in Latin, the language of the empire, and Greek, the language of the culture (John 19:20). The crucifixion is the enthronement of Jesus, his being lifted up from the earth, the moment of royal glory.

Reflection and discussion

• Who are the most powerful people I know? What is the source of their power?

• How is the power of Jesus a stark contrast to worldly power?

• What does Jesus tell Pilate about his kingdom (John 18:36–37)? Who is included in it?

• What power have I been given as a follower of Christ? Do I use the power given to me?

• Who would put Jesus to death in our century? What would be the charge against him?

Prayer

Jesus, king of all God's people, the source of your power is divine truth manifested in love. Reign in my life so that your truth and your justice may characterize all that I say and do. Help me claim the power you share with me and use that power for your glory.

"Very truly, I tell you, before Abraham was, I am." John 8:58

I Am

JOHN 8:23–30 ²³ *He said to them, "You are from below, I am from above; you are of this world, I am not of this world.* ²⁴ *I told you that you would die in your sins, for you will die in your sins unless you believe that I am he."* ²⁵ *They said to him, "Who are you?" Jesus said to them, "Why do I speak to you at all?* ²⁶ *I have much to say about you and much to condemn; but the one who sent me is true, and I declare to the world what I have heard from him."* ²⁷ *They did not understand that he was speaking to them about the Father.* ²⁸ *So Jesus said, "When you have lifted up the Son of Man, then you will realize that I am he, and that I do nothing on my own, but I speak these things as the Father instructed me.* ²⁹ *And the one who sent me is with me; he has not left me alone, for I always do what is pleasing to him."* ³⁰ *As he was saying these things, many believed in him.*

JOHN 18:4–9 ⁴ *Then Jesus, knowing all that was to happen to him, came forward and asked them, "Whom are you looking for?"* ⁵ *They answered, "Jesus of Nazareth." Jesus replied, "I am he." Judas, who betrayed him, was standing with them.* ⁶ *When Jesus said to them, "I am he," they stepped back and fell to the ground.* ⁷ *Again he asked them, "Whom are you looking for?" And they said, "Jesus of Nazareth."* ⁸ *Jesus answered, "I told you that I am he. So if you are looking for me, let these men go."* ⁹ *This was to fulfill the word that he had spoken, "I did not lose a single one of those whom you gave me."*

The name I Am for Jesus occurs throughout the gospel of John, intending this name to identify Jesus with God himself. That I Am as an expression of the divine presence is based on Exodus 3:14, where God reveals himself as "I am who I am." Prophetic passages, especially from Isaiah, also express God's self-revelation in this form; for example Isaiah 43:10, "You are my witnesses... that you may know and believe me and understand that I am he," and Isaiah 45:18, "I am the Lord, and there is no other." In these and many other Old Testament passages, the Hebrew for "I am he" and "I am the Lord" is translated into Greek by "I am."

The way that God revealed himself to his people in the Old Testament is used by Jesus in the gospel to reveal himself as divine. Through this divine title, Jesus defines himself as the one in whom the God of Exodus is present to save once again. Yet, the saving journey on which Jesus will lead his followers ends in life that is eternal.

John's use of the name I Am occurs in some of the most significant passages in which Jesus is revealing who he is. The frightened disciples see someone coming toward them across the waters, and Jesus assures them, "It is I (literally, I Am), do not be afraid" (John 6:20). This is reminiscent of many manifestations of God in the Hebrew Scriptures in which the ones who receive the revelation are told not to fear. In response to the question, "Who are you" (John 8:25), Jesus reveals his intimate relationship with the Father and answers, "When you have lifted up the Son of Man, then you will realize that I am he (literally, I Am)" (John 8:28).

One of the most astounding passages of the gospel occurs as the origins of Jesus are being discussed by his opponents: Jesus said, "Very truly, I tell you, before Abraham was, I am" (John 8:58). This is nothing less than a proclamation that Jesus is divine and existed before all of God's saving works.

The final designation of Jesus as the divine I Am is found at his arrest. Even here, the divine majesty of Jesus is made evident: "When Jesus said to them "I am he (literally, I Am)," they turned away and fell to the ground" (18:6). Surely this response of fear and awe on the part of the soldiers and temple police was due to more than Jesus' simple self-identification as the one they are looking for. Truly this is the presence of the one who had said, "The Father and I are one" (John 10:30).

Reflection and discussion

• Why is I Am a name that fills the listener with awe and reverence?

• What is my greatest fear? Do I trust the words of Jesus, "Do not be afraid," when I am confronted with peril?

• How is the divine majesty of Jesus evident in the world?

Prayer

Jesus, you are the very presence and manifestation of God on earth. Reveal your divine presence to me as I read and meditate on the word of God. Free me from fear and lead me to the fullness of life.

We do not have a high priest who is unable to sympathize with our weaknesses. Heb 4:15

High Priest

HEBREWS 4:14–5:10 ¹⁴*Since, then, we have a great high priest who has passed through the heavens, Jesus, the Son of God, let us hold fast to our confession.* ¹⁵*For we do not have a high priest who is unable to sympathize with our weaknesses, but we have one who in every respect has been tested as we are, yet without sin.* ¹⁶*Let us therefore approach the throne of grace with boldness, so that we may receive mercy and find grace to help in time of need.*

5 ¹*Every high priest chosen from among mortals is put in charge of things pertaining to God on their behalf, to offer gifts and sacrifices for sins.* ²*He is able to deal gently with the ignorant and wayward, since he himself is subject to weakness;* ³*and because of this he must offer sacrifice for his own sins as well as for those of the people.* ⁴*And one does not presume to take this honor, but takes it only when called by God, just as Aaron was.*

⁵*So also Christ did not glorify himself in becoming a high priest, but was appointed by the one who said to him,*

"You are my Son,
  today I have begotten you";
⁶*as he says also in another place,*

"You are a priest for ever,
according to the order of Melchizedek."
⁷*In the days of his flesh, Jesus offered up prayers and supplications, with loud*
cries and tears, to the one who was able to save him from death, and he was
heard because of his reverent submission. ⁸*Although he was a Son, he learned*
obedience through what he suffered; ⁹*and having been made perfect, he became*
the source of eternal salvation for all who obey him, ¹⁰*having been designated by*
God a high priest according to the order of Melchizedek.

HEBREWS 9:6–12 ⁶*Such preparations having been made, the priests go*
continually into the first tent to carry out their ritual duties; ⁷*but only the high*
priest goes into the second, and he but once a year, and not without taking the
blood that he offers for himself and for the sins committed unintentionally by the
people. ⁸*By this the Holy Spirit indicates that the way into the sanctuary has not*
yet been disclosed as long as the first tent is still standing. ⁹*This is a symbol of the*
present time, during which gifts and sacrifices are offered that cannot perfect the
conscience of the worshipper, ¹⁰*but deal only with food and drink and various*
baptisms, regulations for the body imposed until the time comes to set things
right.

¹¹*But when Christ came as a high priest of the good things that have come,*
then through the greater and perfect tent (not made with hands, that is, not of
this creation), ¹²*he entered once for all into the Holy Place, not with the blood of*
goats and calves, but with his own blood, thus obtaining eternal redemption.

The dominant name for Christ in the letter to the Hebrews is high priest. The author assumes the Old Testament understanding of priesthood and applies it in a new way to Jesus. The high priest was the mediator between God and humanity; he was the human representative before God for divine matters. "Every high priest chosen from among mortals," the author writes, "is put in charge of things pertaining to God on their behalf" (5:1). Jesus became like us in every way, able to sympathize with our weaknesses, and "tested as we are" (4:15), so that "he might be a merciful and faithful high priest in the service of God, to make a sacrifice of atonement for the sins of the people" (2:17).

As important as it was for ancient Israel, the Jewish priesthood from the line of Aaron had many deficiencies. The priests had only the imperfect sacrifice of animals to offer, they were personally sinful, and their priesthood was temporal because of their own mortality. The priesthood of Jesus is far more transcendent and also more intimate with us than Israel's ancient priesthood. Not only does our high priest, Jesus, share our humanity fully, but he does so without sin (4:15). The priest of the old covenant presented an imperfect sacrifice each year on the Day of Atonement (9:7–9), but Christ offers his own blood for our atonement. Christ, who is "high priest of the good things that have come," passed through "the greater and perfect tent not made with hands" (9:11) into heaven. Christ entered this heavenly temple "not with the blood of goats and calves but with his own blood" (9:12); thus he obtained eternal redemption for us.

The Old Testament priesthood and its many sacrifices are only a "shadow" (10:1) of the priesthood of Christ. The Old Testament image of Christ's priesthood is the mysterious figure of Melchizedek (Gen 14; Ps 110:4): "Having neither beginning of days nor end of life, but resembling the Son of God, he remains a priest for ever" (7:3). The ancient longings for full atonement and reconciliation with God are fulfilled for us in Christ, our new high priest. As perfect priest and perfect sacrificial victim, the redemption he offers us is complete in every way.

Reflection and discussion

• In what ways did Jesus overcome the limitations of the levitical priesthood?

• In what ways is Jesus like me in all things, except for sin?

• What is a mediator? Why do we need a mediator between God and humanity?

• Why is Christ the perfect mediator?

• Why is the sacrifice of Christ eternal, once and for all?

Prayer

Jesus, merciful High Priest, your death on the cross is the perfect sacrifice for the sin of the world. Thank you for pouring out your own blood for me; thank you for the eternal forgiveness you have offered to me.

SUGGESTIONS FOR FACILITATORS, GROUP SESSION 5

1. Welcome group members and ask if anyone has any questions, announcements, or requests.

2. You may want to pray this prayer as a group:

Lord Jesus, as we come weighed down with the cares of the world and the struggles of life, help us realize that you are the Resurrection and the Life, the True Vine, the Cornerstone, King of the Jews, the great I Am, and our new High Priest. You suffered and were tested in every way we are: pain, distress, rejection, poverty, weakness, temptation, and death. Be our model, mentor, and intercessor before the Father, so that we may follow you along the pilgrim road of life. And when our journey is over, welcome us into the glories of your eternal kingdom, where you live and reign with the Father and the Holy Spirit.

3. Ask one or more of the following questions:
   • Which of the names of Jesus most intrigued you from this week's study?

   • How can knowing the names of Jesus help you in your relationship with Jesus and your prayer life?

4. Discuss lessons 19 through 24. Choose one or more of the questions for reflection and discussion from each lesson to talk over as a group.

5. Ask the group members to name one thing they have most appreciated about the way the group has worked during this Bible study. Ask group members to discuss any changes they might suggest in the way the group works in future studies.

6. Invite group members to complete lessons 25 through 30 on their own during the six days before the next meeting. They should write out their own answers to the questions as preparation for next week's session.

7. Challenge the group to listen carefully to the gospel each week and the liturgical prayers of the Church to recognize the many names of Jesus proclaimed.

8. Conclude by praying aloud together the prayer at the end of one of the lessons discussed. You may want to conclude the prayer by asking members to voice prayers of thanksgiving.

"The wedding guests cannot mourn as long as the bridegroom is with them, can they?" Matt 9:15

Bridegroom

MATTHEW 9:14–15 ¹⁴ *Then the disciples of John came to him, saying, "Why do we and the Pharisees fast often, but your disciples do not fast?"* ¹⁵ *And Jesus said to them, "The wedding guests cannot mourn as long as the bridegroom is with them, can they? The days will come when the bridegroom is taken away from them, and then they will fast."*

EPHESIANS 5:25–33 ²⁵ *Husbands, love your wives, just as Christ loved the church and gave himself up for her,* ²⁶ *in order to make her holy by cleansing her with the washing of water by the word,* ²⁷ *so as to present the church to himself in splendor, without a spot or wrinkle or anything of the kind—yes, so that she may be holy and without blemish.* ²⁸ *In the same way, husbands should love their wives as they do their own bodies. He who loves his wife loves himself.* ²⁹ *For no one ever hates his own body, but he nourishes and tenderly cares for it, just as Christ does for the church,* ³⁰ *because we are members of his body.* ³¹ *"For this reason a man will leave his father and mother and be joined to his wife, and the two will become one flesh."* ³² *This is a great mystery, and I am applying it to Christ and the church.* ³³ *Each of you, however, should love his wife as himself, and a wife should respect her husband.*

The marriage of the bride and the bridegroom is a moment of great joy and hope in scenes throughout the Bible. For the young man, the choice of the bride was the key to his future happiness and the continuation of his line. For the young woman, marriage was joyfully anticipated and was the source of her fulfillment. Marriage was life's transitional moment, the beginning of a new life, and a time of great celebration.

Jesus designates himself as the bridegroom when he explains why his disciples were feasting and not fasting. The disciples of John the Baptist had asked Jesus why his own disciples don't fast as a sign of repentance as they themselves do. Jesus replies that fasting is a sign of mourning. Now that he, the bridegroom, has come to claim Israel, his bride, his disciples must join in the wedding feast, symbolized by the meals they frequently enjoyed together (Matt 9:15). Jesus also implies that he is the bridegroom in the parable of the ten bridesmaids who await the arrival of the bridegroom (Matt 25:1–13).

In the Old Testament, the relationship between God and Israel is often described in terms of matrimony. This imagery is particularly developed in the prophets: "As the bridegroom rejoices over the bride, so shall your God rejoice over you" (Isa 62:5). In the rabbinical interpretation of the Song of Songs, the bridegroom is God himself.

The matrimonial image of loving intimacy and commitment is developed by Paul when he speaks of Christ's love for the church. Christ desires that the church be presented to him as a bride "without spot or wrinkle...holy and without blemish" (Eph 5:27). The Genesis ideal of marriage, "a man will leave his father and mother and be joined to his wife" (Eph 5:31), is an image of the unity that Christ desires to share with his people, the church. One of the Bible's last images of Christ, from the book of Revelation, is of Christ as the bridegroom prepared to meet his bride. "For the marriage of the Lamb has come, and his bride has made herself ready" (Rev 19:7). The bride, the church, wears a garment of "fine linen, bright and pure" (Rev 19:8), and the blessed are called to "the marriage supper of the Lamb" (Rev 19:9).

The matrimonial language of the Scriptures demonstrates the joy of our union with Jesus. As bridegroom he rejoices over us, prepares a home for us, and accepts responsibility for our welfare. The relationship between Jesus and his church is one of deep mutual respect, loving intimacy, and fruitfulness.

Reflection and discussion

• What characteristics of the ideal husband does Jesus demonstrate toward his church?

• Which images of marriage most describe my relationship with Christ?

• What type of marriage counseling do I need to better my relationship with Jesus?

Prayer

Jesus, you are the bridegroom who invites us to the wedding feast of your kingdom. Give me a passionate desire to unite my life to you and to relish the joyful love you have for me.

The Word became flesh and lived among us. John 1:14

The Word

JOHN 1:1–14 *¹In the beginning was the Word, and the Word was with God, and the Word was God. ²He was in the beginning with God. ³All things came into being through him, and without him not one thing came into being. What has come into being ⁴in him was life, and the life was the light of all people. ⁵The light shines in the darkness, and the darkness did not overcome it.*

⁶There was a man sent from God, whose name was John. ⁷He came as a witness to testify to the light, so that all might believe through him. ⁸He himself was not the light, but he came to testify to the light. ⁹The true light, which enlightens everyone, was coming into the world.

¹⁰He was in the world, and the world came into being through him; yet the world did not know him. ¹¹He came to what was his own, and his own people did not accept him. ¹²But to all who received him, who believed in his name, he gave power to become children of God, ¹³who were born, not of blood or of the will of the flesh or of the will of man, but of God.

¹⁴And the Word became flesh and lived among us, and we have seen his glory, the glory as of a father's only son, full of grace and truth.

1 JOHN 1:1–3 *¹We declare to you what was from the beginning, what we have heard, what we have seen with our eyes, what we have looked at and touched with our hands, concerning the word of life—²this life was revealed, and* *we have seen it and testify to it, and declare to you the eternal life that was with the Father and was revealed to us— ³we declare to you what we have seen and heard so that you also may have fellowship with us; and truly our fellowship is with the Father and with his Son Jesus Christ.*

When the gospel of John proclaims that "the Word became flesh and lived among us" (John 1:14), it is stating that the fullest and most complete revelation of God occurred in the life and ministry of Jesus Christ. Throughout the Scriptures, the communication of God to his people is called his "word" to them; God's word is the revelation of God's presence and will. This word spoken throughout the Old Testament is a reflection of the Word, who is the fullness of God: "the Word was God" (John 1:1). This Word was with God in the beginning, before God began his creative work, and through this Word all things came into existence: "All things came into being through him" (John 1:1–3).

John's prologue on the Word of God tells us that this awesome Word, who is divine and eternal, "became flesh." The one through whom the world was created became tangible, palpable, human flesh. The Word "lived among us" (1:14), a phrase that is translated literally as "pitched his tent among us," expresses the intimate quality of the divine presence that came to dwell with us in Jesus Christ. The prologue of John's first letter also expresses this earthly humanity of the "Word of life"—what we have heard, seen, and touched (1 John 1:1). John's gospel and the letters of John are testimonies to what the disciples experienced while the Word was among us as Jesus Christ. The purpose of these writings is to share that life so that we can have fellowship with the Father and the Son (1 John 1:3).

This manifestation of God is both the humble, human Jesus and the enfleshed, divine Word; he is the Jesus who walked the streets of our world, and he is the mighty warrior of the book of Revelation: "He is clothed in a robe dipped in blood, and his name is called The Word of God" (Rev 19:13).

In our culture, words often mean less than they should. Words are plentiful today, yet they are often not well-chosen or backed with deeds. Reflecting on the word of God helps us bring integrity to the words we speak. Words are our means of communicating what is most important, of revealing our deepest selves to another. The word of God is creative, "By the word of the Lord the heavens were made" (Ps 33:6), and accomplishes the purpose for which it is sent (Isa 55:10–11). God's complete and perfect Word is Jesus Christ, "full of grace and truth" (John 1:14). In him, God has communicated what is most important and revealed his deepest self to us.

Reflection and discussion

• Why do we long to hear words with inner conviction and integrity?

• How can I fill my daily speech with greater substance, sincerity, zeal, and confidence?

• Why is John 1:14 often called the heart of Christian revelation?

Prayer

Word of God, may my words reflect your grace and truth. The divine word is creative, purposeful, and truthful. Thank you for taking on my humanity in the flesh so that I might have a share in your divinity.

**On his robe and on his thigh he has a name inscribed,
"King of kings and Lord of lords."** Rev 19:16

King of Kings

1 TIMOTHY 6:12–16 ¹² *Fight the good fight of the faith; take hold of the eternal life, to which you were called and for which you made the good confession in the presence of many witnesses.* ¹³ *In the presence of God, who gives life to all things, and of Christ Jesus, who in his testimony before Pontius Pilate made the good confession, I charge you* ¹⁴ *to keep the commandment without spot or blame until the manifestation of our Lord Jesus Christ,* ¹⁵ *which he will bring about at the right time—he who is the blessed and only Sovereign, the King of kings and Lord of lords.* ¹⁶ *It is he alone who has immortality and dwells in unapproachable light, whom no one has ever seen or can see; to him be honor and eternal dominion. Amen.*

REVELATION 19:11–16 ¹¹ *Then I saw heaven opened, and there was a white horse! Its rider is called Faithful and True, and in righteousness he judges and makes war.* ¹² *His eyes are like a flame of fire, and on his head are many diadems; and he has a name inscribed that no one knows but himself.* ¹³ *He is clothed in a robe dipped in blood, and his name is called The Word of God.* ¹⁴ *And* *the armies of heaven, wearing fine linen, white and pure, were following him on white horses.* ¹⁵*From his mouth comes a sharp sword with which to strike down the nations, and he will rule them with a rod of iron; he will tread the wine press of the fury of the wrath of God the Almighty.* ¹⁶*On his robe and on his thigh he has a name inscribed, "King of kings and Lord of lords."*

The title "King of kings," as it is used in the First Letter to Timothy, proclaims the absolute dominion and power of God over all rulers and nations of the earth. In the book of Revelation, this same title is given to the risen Christ. The Lamb is called "Lord of lords and King of kings." He will conquer the ten kings who yield their power and authority to the beast (Rev 17:12–14). Christ is also presented as the rider of the white horse, the one who conquers the powers of evil symbolized by the beast and its followers. His name is "Word of God" (Rev 19:13) and "King of kings and Lord of lords" (Rev 19:16).

Human kings are described throughout the Bible, beginning with the mention of four Mesopotamian kings in Genesis 14:1, and concluding with the reference to "the kings of the earth" who will bring their treasure to the heavenly Jerusalem in Revelation 21:24. Between these are the many kings of Israel and Judah: the ideal David, the splendorous Solomon, Hezekiah and Josiah as models of righteousness, and kings of rival and neighboring kingdoms.

Throughout the ancient Near East, the power, wealth, and splendor of the king reflected that of the nation. The kings of Egypt, Assyria, Babylon, Persia, and Rome far exceeded the might of Solomon. Some of these nations considered their kings to share in the prerogatives of the gods.

The Bible frequently speaks of God's power using the image of a reigning king. God's kingly rule is first introduced in the Song of Moses: "The Lord will reign forever and ever" (Exod 15:18). God reigns eternally over his own people, including the kings of Israel and Judah. God also rules over all the other nations, and in the end, they will all worship him.

In Jesus, human and divine kingship are merged. To name him the "King of kings" means that his kingdom is that of God, that he reigns over all peoples and nations. His is not a kingdom of worldly power and violent might, but a kingdom of justice, truth, and peace. The King of kings welcomes us to give him our allegiance, to proudly bear the name Christian.

Reflection and discussion

• Why have people throughout history bestowed such power, wealth, and splendor upon their kings?

• How is the kingly rule of Christ different from the reigns of "kings of the earth?"

• What aspect of our world do I find it most difficult to believe Christ reigns over?

• In what aspect of my life must I submit to the reign of Christ?

Prayer

King of kings, I give you my faithful allegiance. Demonstrate your royal power in my life today. Establish your reign over those parts of my world that I have not submitted to your rule.

"I am the Alpha and the Omega, the first and the last, the beginning and the end." Rev 22:13

Alpha and Omega

REVELATION 21:1–7 ¹*Then I saw a new heaven and a new earth; for the first heaven and the first earth had passed away, and the sea was no more.* ²*And I saw the holy city, the new Jerusalem, coming down out of heaven from God, prepared as a bride adorned for her husband.* ³*And I heard a loud voice from the throne saying,*

"See, the home of God is among mortals.
He will dwell with them;
they will be his peoples,
and God himself will be with them;
⁴he will wipe every tear from their eyes.
Death will be no more;
mourning and crying and pain will be no more,
for the first things have passed away."

⁵*And the one who was seated on the throne said, "See, I am making all things new." Also he said, "Write this, for these words are trustworthy and true."* ⁶*Then he said to me, "It is done! I am the Alpha and the Omega, the beginning and the end. To the thirsty I will give water as a gift from the spring of the water of life.* ⁷*Those who conquer will inherit these things, and I will be their God and they will be my children."*

REVELATION 22:6–14 ⁶*And he said to me, "These words are trustworthy and true, for the Lord, the God of the spirits of the prophets, has sent his angel to show his servants what must soon take place."*

⁷*"See, I am coming soon! Blessed is the one who keeps the words of the prophecy of this book."*

⁸*I, John, am the one who heard and saw these things. And when I heard and saw them, I fell down to worship at the feet of the angel who showed them to me;* ⁹*but he said to me, "You must not do that! I am a fellow-servant with you and your comrades the prophets, and with those who keep the words of this book. Worship God!"*

¹⁰*And he said to me, "Do not seal up the words of the prophecy of this book, for the time is near.* ¹¹*Let the evildoer still do evil, and the filthy still be filthy, and the righteous still do right, and the holy still be holy."*

¹²*"See, I am coming soon; my reward is with me, to repay according to everyone's work.* ¹³*I am the Alpha and the Omega, the first and the last, the beginning and the end."*

¹⁴*Blessed are those who wash their robes, so that they will have the right to the tree of life and may enter the city by the gates.*

One of the most exalted names for God and for Jesus in the Bible comes at its conclusion: "I am the Alpha and the Omega" (Rev 1:8; 21:6; 22:13). Alpha and Omega are the first and last letters of the Greek alphabet. In fact, our word "alphabet" comes from the first two letters of the Greek alphabet, alpha and beta. The title, Alpha and Omega is parallel with the description of Jesus as "the first and the last" and "the beginning and the end." The title proclaims the divinity of Christ; he is one with the eternal God.

In Isaiah, God declares: "I am the first and I am the last; besides me there is no god" (Isa 44:6; 48:12). Likewise, at the beginning of Revelation, God declares himself to be the Alpha and the Omega, "who is and who was and who is to come" (Rev 1:8). Like the eternal God, "Jesus Christ is the same yesterday and today and forever" (Heb 13:8).

The letters of the Greek alphabet are used to build words, to communicate with people. Jesus Christ is the alphabet of God's revelation to us. If we want to know God, we have to know Jesus. The ministry of Jesus is to reveal God to us;

he is God's final and complete Word. As the Alpha and Omega, he reveals the mind and heart of God so that we might know God and share eternal life in him.

Most of us tend to procrastinate, and we often leave important things undone. Most of our lives are filled with "unfinished business." But the title Alpha and Omega reminds us that whatever God begins, he finishes. The book of Revelation is the completion of the book of Genesis. In Genesis God created the heavens and the earth; in Revelation, God reveals the new and perfect heaven and earth. In Genesis, Satan began to act, humanity lost paradise, and sin and death began to reign. In Revelation, Satan is bound, paradise is regained, and sin and death are destroyed. God completes his work through Christ, the Alpha and the Omega.

We can be assured that what God has begun in creating each one of us will be brought to completion as he welcomes us home forever. What Jesus started with us in baptism, he will conclude for us in eternal life.

Reflection and discussion

• What work have I begun that I need to bring to a conclusion?

• How can I let Christ be the Alpha of each morning and the Omega of each night of my life?

Prayer

Alpha and Omega, you are the revelation of God; you bring to completion everything you begin. Help me believe that your plan for my life will be completed as I live each day in you.

"I am the bright morning star." Rev 22:16

Morning Star

2 PETER 1:16–19 [16]*For we did not follow cleverly devised myths when we made known to you the power and coming of our Lord Jesus Christ, but we had been eyewitnesses of his majesty.* [17]*For he received honor and glory from God the Father when that voice was conveyed to him by the Majestic Glory, saying, "This is my Son, my Beloved, with whom I am well pleased."* [18]*We ourselves heard this voice come from heaven, while we were with him on the holy mountain.*

[19]*So we have the prophetic message more fully confirmed. You will do well to be attentive to this as to a lamp shining in a dark place, until the day dawns and the morning star rises in your hearts.*

REVELATION 22:16–21 [16]*"It is I, Jesus, who sent my angel to you with this testimony for the churches. I am the root and the descendant of David, the bright morning star."*

[17]*The Spirit and the bride say, "Come."*
And let everyone who hears say, "Come."
And let everyone who is thirsty come.
Let anyone who wishes take the water of life as a gift.

[18]*I warn everyone who hears the words of the prophecy of this book: if anyone adds to them, God will add to that person the plagues described in this book;* [19]*if anyone takes away from the words of the book of this prophecy, God will take away that person's*

share in the tree of life and in the holy city, which are described in this book.
²⁰The one who testifies to these things says, "Surely I am coming soon." Amen.
Come, Lord Jesus! ²¹The grace of the Lord Jesus be with all the saints. Amen.

In 2 Peter and Revelation Jesus is called the morning star. This is the star that shines brightly as the dawn is breaking. The morning star was honored as divine in ancient Middle East and Greco-Roman religions. As this star signals the breaking of dawn, Christ signals the beginning of a new age.

Matthew's gospel tells us that the coming of Jesus is like a light in the darkness, fulfilling the words of Isaiah: "The people who sat in darkness have seen a great light, and for those who sat in the region and shadow of death light has dawned" (Matt 4:16). Luke's gospel describes the coming of Christ: "the dawn from on high will break upon us" (Luke 1:78). After a long night of longing and expectation, Jesus is that bright hope on the horizon.

Throughout the Bible, stars are regarded as among the most glorious of God's creatures. In recounting God's works, the psalmist sings, "He determines the number of the stars; he gives to all of them their names" (Ps 147:4). In comparing our earthly bodies with risen bodies, Paul says that "star differs from star in glory" (1 Cor 15:41).

In antiquity, people believed that a new star marked the birth of a new ruler. An ancient prophecy in Israel said that "a star shall come out of Jacob" (Num 24:17), a passage that was later understood to refer to the messianic king who would come from the tribe of Judah. The star that marked the birth of Jesus (Matt 2:2) was understood to be a fulfillment of this ancient prophecy given to Moses.

The second letter of Peter speaks about the future glorious coming of Christ. Readers are urged to be attentive to the prophecies of Christ's coming "until the day dawns and the morning star rises in your hearts" (2 Pet 1:19). Christ is that "bright morning star" (Rev 22:16) whose rising signals the coming day.

We can better understand the term "superstar" as a metaphor for Christ today. It is a term we use for contemporary heroes and celebrities. Even Jesus has been called Superstar in recent culture. The bright morning star was the superstar of the ancient world. We look to Jesus as our guiding star, as sailors look to a star to guide their journey. He is a sure guide in the midst of darkness, confusion, and frustration. He is our morning star who pierces the night and assures us that a new day is beginning.

Reflection and discussion

• What hour of the day is best for me as a time for quiet prayer? What parts of the natural world enhance my prayer at that hour?

• How do the star-studded sky and the sunrise remind me of the glories of Christ?

• What new light can Christ bring into my darkness today?

Prayer

Bright Morning Star, you signal the dawn of my salvation. Help me look to you as the hope of each new day. Increase my trust in your power to raise me to eternal life.

Everyone who calls on the name of the Lord shall be saved. Rom 10:13

The Lord

ROMANS 10:5–13 *⁵Moses writes concerning the righteousness that comes from the law, that "the person who does these things will live by them." ⁶But the righteousness that comes from faith says, "Do not say in your heart, 'Who will ascend into heaven?'" (that is, to bring Christ down) ⁷"or 'Who will descend into the abyss?'" (that is, to bring Christ up from the dead). ⁸But what does it say?*

"The word is near you,
on your lips and in your heart"

(that is, the word of faith that we proclaim); ⁹because if you confess with your lips that Jesus is Lord and believe in your heart that God raised him from the dead, you will be saved. ¹⁰For one believes with the heart and so is justified, and one confesses with the mouth and so is saved. ¹¹The scripture says, "No one who believes in him will be put to shame."

¹²For there is no distinction between Jew and Greek; the same Lord is Lord of all and is generous to all who call on him. ¹³For, "Everyone who calls on the name of the Lord shall be saved."

PHILIPPIANS 2:5–11 *⁵Let the same mind be in you that was in Christ Jesus,*
⁶who, though he was in the form of God,
did not regard equality with God
as something to be exploited,

108

⁷but emptied himself,
    taking the form of a slave,
    being born in human likeness.
And being found in human form,
⁸he humbled himself
    and became obedient to the point of death—
    even death on a cross.
⁹Therefore God also highly exalted him
    and gave him the name
    that is above every name,
¹⁰so that at the name of Jesus
    every knee should bend,
    in heaven and on earth and under the earth,
¹¹and every tongue should confess
    that Jesus Christ is Lord,
    to the glory of God the Father.

The title Lord is used so commonly for Jesus throughout the New Testament that we may hardly take note of its significance. Yet it is the most exalted title given to Jesus, the name above all others, referring to his risen glory and his sovereign authority at the right hand of his Father.

A powerful image of Christ's lordship looks to Psalm 110:1 where King David sings: "The Lord says to my lord, 'Sit at my right hand.'" In the gospels, Jesus asks how the Messiah could be David's son if David calls him "lord" (Matt 22:41–45). The implication is that, even though the Messiah is the son of David by blood, he is also the lord of David. God invites him to sit at the place of honor at the right of God's throne, implying that he shares in God's authority over the earth.

When the Old Testament was translated into Greek, the personal name of God (Hebrew, *YHWH*) was translated by *Kyrios*, the Greek word for Lord. So when the followers of Jesus proclaimed him as Lord, they were implying that Jesus shared in the authority and divinity of the God of Israel. To call Jesus "the Lord" is to praise him as the mighty presence of God come to dwell among us. This fullest meaning of the title is surely affirmed in John's gospel when Thomas says of the Risen Christ, "My Lord and my God!" (John 20:28).

Paul describes a follower of Christ as one who confesses that "Jesus is Lord" (Rom 10:9) and who "calls on the name of the Lord" (Rom 10:13). He recalls the hymn of the early Christians who proclaim Christ as the one who emptied and humbled himself, but whom God exalted (Phil 2:7–9). God bestowed upon him "the name that is above every name" so that at the name of Jesus every knee should bend and every tongue confess that "Jesus Christ is Lord" (Phil 2:11).

"Jesus is Lord" is the earliest creed of the Church. It is rooted in the early Jewish Christians of Jerusalem who prayed in Aramaic, "Marana tha," which means, "Our Lord, come!" (1 Cor 16:22). For the early Christians and for us today, Lord is a title that professes the risen, glorious state of Jesus and his absolute authority over all creation. If Jesus is Lord of our lives, then he is sovereign over all aspects of our lives. The path to all that is noble, holy, and eternal is marked by the lordship of Jesus, so much so that we can urge one another: "Whatever you do, in word or deed, do everything in the name of the Lord Jesus" (Col 3:17).

Reflection and discussion

• Why is Lord the most exalted title for Jesus?

• What does it mean to "do everything in the name of the Lord Jesus" (Col 3:17)? Is it possible for me to do this?

• Is Jesus the Lord of my life? How willing am I to entrust my security, my possessions, and my future to his will?

• The early Christians prayed with watchful anticipation, "Come, Lord Jesus." How could this prayer deepen my longing for Christ?

• In what ways has my study of the names of Jesus helped me to know him?

Prayer

Lord Jesus, the angels of heaven and the people of the earth bend their knees at your holy name. Extend your reign over all parts of my life so that all my words and actions testify that you are Lord.

SUGGESTIONS FOR FACILITATORS, GROUP SESSION 6

1. Welcome group members and make any final announcements or requests.

2. You may want to pray this prayer as a group:

Jesus, you are risen, glorified, and exalted. You have been given the name above every name, so that at your holy name, every knee should bend in heaven and on earth. You are Bridegroom, Word of God, King of kings, Alpha and Omega, Morning Star, and Lord. Your Holy Spirit has inspired your disciples to give you these and numerous names to express your boundless richness. May that same Holy Spirit guide us as we seek to know, imitate, and follow you.

3. Ask one or more of the following questions:

   • How have the names of Jesus helped you to pray?

   • In what way has this study challenged you the most?

4. Discuss lessons 25 through 30. Choose one or more of the questions for reflection and discussion from each lesson to discuss as a group.

5. Ask the group if they would like to study another in the Threshold Bible Study series. Discuss the topic and dates, and make a decision among those interested. Ask the group members to suggest people they would like to invite to participate in the next study series.

6. Ask the group to discuss the insights that stand out most from this study over the past six weeks.

7. Conclude by praying aloud the following prayer or another of your own choosing:

Holy Spirit of the glorified Christ, you inspired the writers of the Scriptures and you have guided our study during these weeks. Continue to deepen our love for the word of God in the holy Scriptures and draw us more deeply into the heart of Jesus. We have each been called by name to follow Jesus. Continue to unite us as disciples so that together we may claim the victory, the redemption, and the new life that he pours out upon us. Bless us with the fire of your love.